# Awakening Transformation

A Beginner's Guide to Becoming Your Higher Self

## Tianna Roser

Infinite Light Books

PO Box 152952

Austin, TX 78715

Cover Designer: Steve Kuhn

Photo Credit: Alicia Leigh Photography

Infinite Light Books

PO Box 152952

Austin, TX 78715

Awakening Transformation/ Tianna Roser. -- 1st ed.

ISBN 978-1-7377053-0-7

# Contents

# Preface

I'm not the kind of person who gets psychic readings....anymore. These days I mostly go within to tap into my higher self or my spirit guide's wisdom. Yet I was intrigued when my friend told me that a medical intuitive was guiding her through a major medical issue. My own lingering health issue seemed to elude the doctor, acupuncturist and naturopath. The inner spiritual guidance I received wasn't very specific. My spirit guide, Will, an evolved non-physical being, only said that I needed to go through this challenge and that I'd be okay.

So I decided to book an hour-long phone session with the intuitive. Thirty minutes in, we'd covered health issues to my satisfaction, but I still had time left. As a sort of psychic Hail Mary, I said, "Can you just ask the guides if there's anything else I need to know?"

"They're saying that you need to write a book. It'll be a beacon of light for certain souls who are meant to find you. It needs to come out in the next one to three years."

Oh man, Spirit was calling me out! You see, this wasn't the first, or second, or even third time Spirit told me to write a book. Many years ago, back when I occasionally consulted with psychics, they consistently told me it was part of my soul's plan to write a book. I tried several times, even going so far as creating my own writing retreat at a charming little Spanish village. I made progress on a couple books, but could never finish one.

Inevitably, I'd ask myself, "Who am I to write a book? Haven't other writers covered this material many times before?"

So I threw that question back to the intuitive and she replied, "You have your own taste of Woo that that certain people need." (Woo refers to "woo woo," meaning metaphysical/spiritual topics.) What she said made sense. It's not about claiming to be an expert. I can just share my insights and experiences to encourage others to keep going on this uncharted path into the unknown.

Alright then. It was time to try writing again but from this new perspective. It'd been years since my last book attempt, but I knew the old half-finished book files were still around somewhere. As I sifted through the documents, I came across a channeled message from my spirit guide Will. More than a decade old, this message about writing a book had completely slipped my mind:

*It is important that you do not worry about redundancy in providing information that others have offered. It will be in your unique organization and approach that you attract your readers. You offer a lightness and a sort of mysticism that appeals to a specific audience, many of whom are in soul contracts with you. You agreed to be their wake up call. They will feel the pull and find your book in various ways. This is one reason that writing a book is so crucial to fulfilling your own mission.*

Mind blown! How had I forgotten that message? It was a strong confirmation that Spirit gently pushes us towards our soul purpose and will keep trying to give us the message through any possible way.

So finally, here it is. Perhaps you are one of the souls who has been waiting for me to fulfill our agreement. If so, I apologize for the delay, but I also believe that everything happens in divine timing. It's a great comfort to realize that Spirit returns again and again to give us the nudge needed to fulfill our soul's purpose! This book isn't designed to be a complete instruction manual for spiritual awakening. It's a simple primer filled with a sprinkling of my experiences on the path. I hope it activates your spiritual fervor and encourages you to persevere despite the inevitable confusion and challenges you'll meet along the way.

# Introduction

Your inner light is awakening. This book attracted you because you are opening to your divinity. The old limiting world of separation is crumbling. Hurray! You're discovering new possibilities you were unaware of only a few years ago. A glorious high vibrational world is opening up, beyond what you can see or touch. However, this expansive spiritual realm can initially be overwhelming.

Let this book be a trusted guide for your spiritual adventure.

Any topic covered here could be a book in itself. Perhaps in the future, I may do that! The intention for this book, however, is to provide a road map as you awaken to your spiritual self. It's not meant to be all-encompassing, but rather, a bird's eye view, highlighting some key tools and concepts to support you in your journey. Read it from start to finish, or pick and choose topics.

Who am I to write a book on spiritual awakening? Consider me your soul sister. I'm sharing my journey to remind you that you're not alone.

My own story of opening to Spirit is perhaps not unlike yours in certain aspects. It began with disillusionment with the world and my place in it.

I've always been sensitive. As a young child, my own emotions and the ability to feel energy overpowered me, expressed as massive temper tantrums. The defining moment was at five years old, when my well-meaning uncle told me a story about trolls that snuck into the bedrooms of little girls who got angry and stole them away, never to be seen again. I remember lying awake at night in my bottom bunk bed terrified to close my eyes, lest the trolls might get me, while my sister slept soundly above.

After that, I had a major personality shift. It wasn't a conscious decision, but I moved out of the treacherous emotional zone into the safety of the mind. I became quieter, less expressive. Years passed in this more reserved manner. In high school, I was basically a good kid, although drinking alcohol at parties enabled me to come out of my shell. I got good grades and participated in many extracurricular activities.

At college I chose to study business. I wasn't passionate about anything, the way that some friends always knew they wanted to be a doctor, lawyer or pilot. I figured the world would always need business people, so it was a completely logical choice. Seemed like the smart thing to do, right? It's crazy how we could possibly think that at nineteen or twenty years old we know ourselves well enough to choose our life's work.

When it was time to choose a Business Administration major, my thought process was, 'Well I don't like numbers, so I guess I'll choose Marketing.' I got the Marketing internship I wanted, which led to a job offer. Finally, I made it! All my hard work had led me exactly where I planned. So why was I so dissatisfied?

The corporate world felt fake and soulless, not that I believed in souls then. I was raised as an atheist. Admittedly, in college I was one of those wanna-be intellectuals who mocked the campus Christian Jesus lovers. How pathetic, I thought, that anyone could believe there's an old man in the sky that they need to please? How deluded are people to think God had one son who only came to Earth once and died two thousand years ago to atone for everyone's sins? Harsh, right? I still don't believe in that particular limited version of God and Jesus, but I've grown to respect others' beliefs. We are each following our own unique path.

Money never motivated me. Yet, without awareness of a higher purpose, I assumed career success must be the pinnacle of life. Here I was, starting my career and on a successful path, yet I felt empty. I saw the office politics, the corporate greed, the time and energy drain in unnecessarily long, inefficient workdays in an unhealthy environment, and I began to wonder, what's the point? Does this even matter? Why stress myself out to make some company a ton of money and earn a more impressive job title just so I can accumulate nicer stuff? When I'm dead, what will my life purpose have been?

This existential crisis began to unravel everything I thought I knew. It led me to question EVERY SINGLE THING. Who am I? What do I truly want? What fulfills me? I began to look for answers outside the conventional path I'd always trusted and followed. Down the rabbit hole I went.

I led a double life. I spent weekdays pretending to carry on the corporate charade and weekends doing psychedelics, hanging out with other nonconformists, and dancing to electronic music at the rave scene. Psychedelics opened me to other realms. The Oneness I felt in these experiences awakened a memory of the truth - that we're all connected. Those psychedelic experiences felt more real than the games we play and the masks we wear in our 3D lives. An insatiable thirst for mystical knowledge emerged. I spent all my free time in used bookstores, buried under a stack of metaphysical books. I finally found the passion I'd been yearning for.

Unbeknownst to me, a big spiritual awakening was stirring within.

A few years before my first major spiritual initiation, I had a powerful dream. I was still in overachiever mode, working three part time jobs while taking a full semester of college classes. I was too busy to realize how drained I was. Perhaps you're familiar with carrying the heaviness from the world's drudgery. A dark cloud hung in my mind. Why did life have to be so hard?

One night I dreamt I was walking wearily near a busy road. The landscape was dry and bleak. My sore, tired legs felt ready to give out. Meanwhile, my friends happily whizzed by in sports cars, laughing and partying. Resigned to the tedious journey, I accepted that I must walk it by myself.

Out of the corner of my eye, I noticed green shrubbery that ran alongside my path. Suddenly, out popped a figure from behind the bushes. Somehow I knew it was my spirit guide. Indescribable joy filled me as I realized the aloneness was an illusion I had chosen for my growth! No one was forcing me to walk. I knew that traveling a different route from the pack, a seemingly harder way, would give me the genuine fulfillment I was seeking. This dream was my own version of the "Footprints in the Sand" poem. It remains fresh in my mind after all these years, strengthening me in hard times.

Years later when I was going through the darkest period of my life, I channeled this message from Will:

*I am still here with you, as I have always been throughout time and in all your lifetimes, although many passed by without your awareness of this support and connection. Never fear that I've abandoned or neglected you. I love you immensely and would never choose this, even if it were possible. Remember that we are all connected and it's impossible to be abandoned. Separation is the greatest illusion, but a powerful teacher. You must remember that you have chosen a growth-oriented path in this lifetime.*

*Remember the feeling as a child when you would tell your parents "I can do this." And they said "Not yet, you're still a baby." I wish to remind you that you are no longer a baby. I believe in you and therefore I step aside and allow you to stumble and fall a bit as you figure things out on your own. At times it can feel very lonely, but it's all an illusion. You need that aloneness to gain a sense of accomplishment in figuring it out yourself. You are not one who likes to be babied or condescended in any way.*

*Sometimes life feels tough because that was the route you chose, not because no one cares. Remind yourself of this distinction often. You are so loved and cherished. It can be no other way. Don't let appearances fool you. There is so much love pouring out to you. Make time to receive it through meditation or energy work. Nothing has been lost.*

Since that dream, my life has transformed. I've undertaken a powerful journey that led me to communicate with my spirit guide, connected me with my soul family, awakened unconditional love within, and activated my higher consciousness.

This book helps you take a similar journey. It provides you with tools to first Know Your Self, Love Your Self, and Empower Your Self, so that finally you can Become Your Higher Self. I capitalize the world Self when I'm referring to your true self rather than the limited personality self. Throughout the book I also use the terms "higher self" and "soul" interchangeably to mean your eternal spiritual essence that exists beyond this one lifetime.

I hope this content helps you on your spiritual ascension path and encourages you to push forward when the journey weighs you down and wears you out. As you step into this new Aquarian Age, you are supported in awakening to your highest potential.

# Why Are You Here?

Let's start by getting the biggest question out of the way.

Why Are You Here?

## The Journey from Oneness to Individuality

In the Beginning....(Dun, Dun, Dun)...there was just the Oneness, the All That Is. The Oneness, being everything, wanted to know itself more distinctly, so it separated into different parts.

To understand this more clearly, let's imagine that your body is the Oneness. Curl your body up into a ball, so that all your parts are now just one blob. Wrapped up tightly, it's hard to differentiate the parts of you. Now stretch and fully extend your body. You can begin to notice your fingers or knee as they separate from the rest of your body. You can recognize how each part varies in contrast to another part.

Each body part has a different size, shape, and function. No part is better or worse than another. They all contribute to the whole, but in unique ways. There's beauty in the body parts' diversity and the way they connect and interact with each other.

Imagine that each of these parts of the All That Is is a soul, a little piece of the One. To know each specific part, you (the Oneness) decided to incarnate into the illusion of separation. You've chosen to manifest as a singular human on Earth and forget that you are Everything, so that you can understand what it's like to be one unique thing.

Let's say you chose in this lifetime to be born into a female body, which provides experiences exclusive to this body type. How unfair and how limited it would be if you only had one shot at incarnation and never experienced the perspective of being in a male body! To fully know yourself, you choose to return again and again, trying out all the possibilities in gender, race, sexual orientation, body type, socioeconomic status and more.

You agreed to incarnate into the limitations of time and space, which give the illusion of separation and veil your awareness that you are the Oneness. For if you remembered being Everything from the start of your life, it might be difficult to focus on just being one specific thing. Imagine if in your last life you had a big strong masculine body. In this lifetime, you chose a petite feminine body. If you still identified with your former body, it would be challenging to adapt to this tiny body and fully appreciate its unique qualities.

# Karma Is a Tool for Growth

It helps to come into each life with a fresh mind, with no old memories clouding your perception. However, even though you don't remember the details of your former lives, you still carry over unresolved energy from the past known as karma. Let's clear up a major misconception: Karma is not a reward and punishment system.

Sometimes in a past life regression my client says, "My life has been so painful. I want to know what bad things I did in a past life to deserve this karma." Karma doesn't work like that. There's no one handing out karma based on your worthiness. Karma is much like Newton's third law of motion: for every action there is an equal and opposite reaction. There is no judgment of good or bad. It's just energy. What's showing up in your life as karma is simply the resulting energy of what you put into motion previously, whether in this life or a past life.

Karma is energy that offers you the gift of awareness once you transform it through processing it. Most people process karma through living it. The karmic energy magnetizes people and events to you that allow you to face it and work through it. If you don't get the lesson the first time, the energy remains unshifted within you and will continue to attract new opportunities to transform it. Surely you've encountered this in your life already: leaving one situation (relationship, job, living place) and then finding yourself with the same problems in a new situation. Karma can make life feel like the movie "Groundhog Day," where it's the same thing repeated over and over and there's no escape.

Karma doesn't have to be a life sentence! The other way to clear karma is to discover it inwardly and transmute it through any number of consciousness practices, such as the ones listed in this book. Once you unlock the lesson embedded in the karma, the energy shifts into a higher vibration. You'll now attract experiences into your life that match this new frequency, things that tend to be more enjoyable.

So these lifetimes have been wildly enriching, but you're beginning to wonder, how do you move beyond an endless reincarnation cycle?

# The Soul's Evolution Through Reincarnation

I highly recommend reading "Journey of Souls" by Michael Newton, based on hypnotic regression case studies exploring the soul's experiences between incarnations. It provides an essential framework to understand how you evolve as a soul over many lifetimes. This book was so inspiring, I decided to get certified in hypnosis and in Life Between Lives Regression with the Michael Newton Institute. Newton was able to construct a map of the soul's evolution based on consistent reports from thousands of his clients' sessions.

When you left the awareness of being All That Is and began your journey incarnating, you chose to experience complete spiritual amnesia so that you could truly understand what it's like to be an individual body. This limited awareness is like being thrown into a dark room and trying to navigate your way. Initially you're disoriented, stumbling around and bumping into others, harming them or they harm you. You're adapting to the physical body. Due to the veil of forgetfulness, you think you are just a body and experience the world through this very focused but limited awareness.

At this "baby soul awareness" level, the body's needs, wants and desires drive you. It's natural that babies are selfish; they fixate on getting their needs met. Yet you don't judge babies for this. You understand that this is a normal stage in every person's development. Similarly, you mustn't judge "baby souls" for only focusing only on themselves. We all start off at this stage in our evolution.

A big mistake many make is judging others as if everyone is at the same level of awareness and should know better. You wouldn't get angry with a second grader who didn't know Calculus. You recognize that's beyond their development level. In the same way, how can you be upset that someone's actions hurt your feelings, when they aren't at the development level to know any better?

I'm not excusing perpetrators, but this understanding will help you heal and forgive when you understand that nothing is personal. People's actions reflect their awareness level. You can't force someone to grow their awareness, but you can learn to discern who to stay clear of. (More on that later!) Also, try not to assume you know what anyone else's grade level is. The beggar on the street corner could be a highly evolved soul. The world leader could be a baby soul. It's best to accept that it's none of your business what other souls are here to learn. Your soul has a blueprint of what it came in to learn, so focus on that and enjoy the journey!

In your early incarnations, your consciousness is mostly veiled, but you learn and grow through the trial and error of making choices and living out the consequences. All awareness gained through this process remains after that life finishes. In your next incarnation, although you return into forgetfulness of what happened prior, you retain the consciousness you gained in previous lives.

To grossly oversimplify it, just imagine that in your initial incarnation, your energy body was 95% dark (lack of awareness) and 5% light (spiritual awareness.) In each incarnation, you are increasing your light due to your consciousness awakening in the Earth School. You may learn the hard way that murder is not a good idea, but loyalty is worthwhile. There are an extensive number of themes to explore, which is why we come back again and again. Just one area of study, such as balancing the needs of others and the needs of yourself, could take numerous lifetimes to fully understand.

In some lifetimes you may choose to take on a heavy load because you want to grow quickly. You may make a big leap in your light quantity in just one life. Other incarnations may be a vacation life, where you just want to relax and recover from a difficult previous life. There's no judgment about how long it takes for you to grow. Time doesn't really exist in Spirit. Time and space are constructs we utilize on Earth to help us experience separation and explore cause and effect. From the soul's perspective, you have however much time you need to return home to Oneness.

As you move further along in your evolution, your energy body constitutes more light than dark. You'll naturally begin to focus spiritually, simply because you resonate with the light of consciousness. The fact that you're even interested in this book means that you are not a baby soul. Newer souls are fascinated with the outer reality, while an older soul tends to be introspective and self aware.

Finally, after many lifetimes. you'll fully embody your soul's consciousness and complete your journey of incarnating into physical form. As some say, you'll exit the Wheel of Rebirth. Whew - what a ride, right? What happens then, I can't say for sure. The next spiritual adventure will await you. Don't concern yourself with that just yet. There's still so much to explore in the here and now. In fact, you chose for this lifetime to incarnate during a powerful time of dynamic shift on Earth.

# The Shift

You live in a potent era of rapid transformation. This civilization's old power structures are dismantling before your eyes, which is quite frightening to some. In the past, many people opted for the stability of what's known, but unhealthy, over what's unknown, yet possibly amazing. Nowadays, there really is no choice anymore. It's not possible to stay in the lower vibrations, pretending not to see the dysfunction and imbalance within yourself and in our world. All the toxic beliefs and behaviors are coming up to heal and clear because they're unsustainable in the higher energies now prevalent on Earth. It's akin to a collective energy detox. Major change is past due on the planet. Our disconnection to Earth and to our own self has led to an imbalanced way of life. Eventually nature always restores balance. That time is now.

The vibration on the planet is increasing. As Mother Earth goes through her alchemical transmutation from lower to higher density, all life here must do the same. Some people aptly call this time "The Quickening" because everything is speeding up, including your spiritual awakening. This tends to intensify this process. It's challenging to stabilize yourself in a fast, changing world. Be compassionate to yourself, yet also remember that you chose to incarnate in this highly exciting time. You have unprecedented potential to accelerate your spiritual development. What previously took lifetimes to achieve can now take place in years or even just months!

Here's a message from Will on The Shift:

*The planet is undergoing its own spiritual awakening, as you all are undergoing a similar process individually. Individually you are shifting at different paces, suitable for your own growth level at your own speed of assimilation of energies. There are increasingly higher fluctuations of frequencies on the planet and each of you process these energies as best you can.*

*Those who embrace this shift and do practices that are aligned with opening and clearing energetic pathways within, such as yoga, meditation, martial arts, breathing practices, energy work or alternative healing modalities, will find that this high vibrational energy is creating rapid shifts within and in your outer life. Those who resist change and shut themselves off from the energetic flow will find life becoming more difficult to navigate until at some point they let go of the old ways that no longer work in the new energies.*

*All will experience waves of energy, highs and lows. Accept the fluctuations as part of the experience. Do not become attached to any point in time. Learning to ride the waves is part of the growth opportunity presented at this time. Do not place your sense of security and well-being in fixed outer situations, rather, gain stability from your own inner connection. This will give you ease and confidence that you can navigate any changes presented in the days ahead.*

*You may feel distressed at times as you notice the disarray in the world around you. You are doing the best you can in the world you live in, helping those around you and affecting change when you can. Be the hope and inspiration for others. Feelings of helplessness only reinforce that energy in the world. There will continue to be uprisings, dis-*

*array and shifts occurring, as old ways of being need to be healed. Consider it the world's growing pains.*

*Don't focus on the outer world of your physical senses. Keep connecting within and bringing the divine love here to the physical embodiment. It starts with you. Be conscious of holding and expressing love energy whenever possible, even to strangers. Every day, big or small opportunities present themselves so that you may offer more love to the world. Keep this focus and remember that only love can heal darkness.*

# CHAPTER 2

# Know Yourself

The spiritual awakening path is a journey to know your Self, the authentic you - beyond your body, your life experiences, your family, your culture. The authentic Self is the you that has always existed. It's the you beyond time and space. A big part of who you think you are is actually a composite of these outside influences that have shaped you in this life. And while that is an aspect of you, there is a much greater you waiting to be uncovered. The practices in this chapter will assist you in becoming acquainted with the eternal unique essence that is You.

## Focus Within: Meditate

By now, most everyone is aware of the benefits of meditation. All the cool kids are doing it, from CEOs to rock stars. Yet I constantly hear from my clients: "I tried meditation but it's too hard." "I'm frustrated." "I meditate but I don't think I'm doing it right. I don't feel that different."

I totally get that! I too was frustrated when I first started meditating. It was so challenging to quiet my busy mind. I tried and gave up numerous times before something finally clicked. If it wasn't for my spirit guide lovingly insisting that he would only connect with me through meditation, I would've given up completely.

Initially I attempted to sit still and simply empty my mind. This is perhaps the most difficult way to learn meditation! People often have the misconception that you're only meditating properly if you experience long periods of inner silence. While certainly that's wonderful and possible, it's also perfectly normal to have thoughts coming in and out during meditation. The key is not to engage with the thought. Just let it pass through and bring your attention back to the present moment.

Understandably, that's not easy to do at first.

What worked for me was listening to guided meditation audios. Amazingly, when someone else was talking, my mind would be quiet and listen. I would listen to an hour long guided meditation. It took that whole time just to settle my busy mind. After that, I just wanted to stay in that incredible peace. I would end up meditating three to four hours at a time! I meditated after work, so I didn't put any limit on my sessions. In that deep state, time didn't exist. It didn't feel long at all.

Looking back, I'd say that regularly meditating for several hours a day is a surefire recipe for spiritual awakening. In those few hours, a whole new world opened up. I began feeling energy sensations like tingling and warmth during meditation. I went through a period where, after that initial hour, I would somehow slip out of my body and be floating in the Cosmos. I was spontaneously traveling into past lives even though I wasn't sure if I believed in reincarnation. It was a complete paradigm shift.

Meditation was (and is) an indispensable tool in my spiritual toolkit. I'm not suggesting that everyone should try to meditate for several hours a day. I don't have time to do that anymore, nor do I feel it's right for me to meditate that long at this point on my path. I needed those big experiences initially to trust in this inner world. I tend to be someone who likes the big "knock me over the head" experience, while that would overwhelm other people. You have your unique path. It's important not to compare your spiritual journey to others.

Meditation isn't really about these cool fantastical experiences I'm sharing. Those are sometimes a by-product of the practice, but they're not the purpose of it.

Meditation teaches you to just be in this moment, without expectations or judgment. It's hard not to question whether you're doing it correctly or whether this is what you're "supposed to feel." Yet, there isn't really any "supposed to" with meditation. It's simply a practice in awareness and in noticing anything that takes you out of present moment awareness. Certainly you can have big emotions come up or powerful insights. More likely though, you'll experience subtle benefits: relaxation, centeredness, peace of mind. It's easy to miss these quiet inner benefits when you're used to the noise and flashiness of everything in the outer world.

This is precisely why you need to meditate. Our modern world is overrun by corporations that compete for your attention to fill your mind with their messages. To definitively know who you are, you need some time to turn your focus inward and discover what's authentically you, without the influence of anyone else. Don't worry, I'm not suggesting that you unplug from society and live off the grid. Although that sounds kinda nice, doesn't it? It's just not realistic for most of us, nor is it necessary. Gone are the days when following a spiritual path meant living alone in a cave on a mountain. If you've been practicing for a while without experiencing any subtle benefits, such as feeling calmer, more at ease and balanced, then it's probably time to try another technique.

There are tons of different meditation techniques. I don't believe there is one best way to meditate. Try a number of methods (mindfulness, mantra meditation, transcendental meditation, loving kindness meditation, moving meditation, etc.) until you find one that matches you and your temperament. Whatever type you'll stick to is the best one for you.

Here's a message from Will on Meditation with Ease:

*Meditation is the process of being aware in the present moment, as well as the process of catching yourself when you are not in the present. No one is likely to maintain their awareness in the present all the time. It is neither easy nor necessary to your growth. If you wish to further develop your meditation practice for your personal and spiritual* growth, simply notice what emotions come up during and after your meditation practice. Afterward, reflect on these emotions.

Do you feel frustration or annoyance for not being able to maintain constant awareness? Do you feel happy after a "good" meditation? Sad or angry after a "not so great" meditation? Emotional patterns that arise during your meditation are reflections of your overall patterns. You can discover tendencies for worry, fear, perfectionism, or anything that keeps you from fully and completely accepting yourself and the situation in the moment. Simply in recognizing the pattern and becoming aware of it, you bring light to it. In that awareness you now have the power to release this emotion, thought or belief and just accept and allow what is.

You already have the mechanics of meditation down. There are many different ways to do the same practice, none better or worse. Choose a meditation method that you enjoy, one that brings excitement rather than drudgery. Some people can use the same method their entire life, others will want to change from time to time to feel refreshed.

You can try meditation with music, following your breath, or walking meditation - just to name a few. The method itself does not matter. The mechanics remain the same. The way you utilize the meditation and incorporate it into your whole day, or your whole life, is what is most valuable. Find a method you delight in. Enjoy the process of being aware, as well as the process of coming back to awareness. Enjoy the process of accepting yourself as you are right now, as well as the process of ever-changing and growing.

# Connect to Your Higher Self and Spirit Guides

Communicating with your higher self and spirit guides is one of the most exciting tools available for your spiritual development. If you'd like assistance with the process of connecting with your spiritual team, you can listen to guided meditations for meeting your spirit guides or book a session with a certified hypnotist like myself. Or you could do what I did: I started working with my own guides by learning how to channel.

Channeling is the process of opening yourself to allow spiritual beings to communicate through you. It has received a lot of hype and criticism over the years, but nonetheless is effective for connecting to higher wisdom. Channeling is simply a form of self-hypnosis or meditation.

## Don't Try This at Home

Channeling played a pivotal role in my own spiritual activation. I'd always been a vivid dreamer, so my boyfriend at the time, Max, gifted me with a book on dreaming. As it turned out, this book was channeled by a non-physical being named Seth. Seth was a delightful wellspring of metaphysical knowledge. He explained the nature of physical reality and the Universe in new ways that inspired me. I envied the author, Jane Roberts, the channel of Seth. What would it be like to have Seth just a thought away, available to answer the deepest questions of our existence?

Well, if Jane Roberts had a wise spirit guide, couldn't it be possible that we all do? I wondered if I could contact my own Seth. I devoured every Seth book I could get my hands on. In one of them, Ms. Roberts detailed the story of her first contact with Seth. It was through a Ouija board!

Wait, what? Where does a person even obtain a Ouija board? The funny thing was that I found it in the board game section of a toy store, right alongside Monopoly and Clue. How could it be that this cardboard and plastic game manufactured in a factory in China could be the key to connecting me to my spirit guide? I didn't have a better idea, so I decided to try it out.

Max wasn't necessarily on the same spiritual path as me, but he was an open-minded guy. He agreed to try the Ouija Board out with me. From the first time we placed our hands on the plastic triangle, it moved wildly, spelling out gibberish. Whereas the average person would consider that a failure, I actually felt encouraged by the strong movement. We set out to practice daily. Soon enough it began to spell out words.

We were communicating with a spirit! Let's call him Bob. Excitedly I asked, "Are you my spirit guide?" The pointer moved to No. "Do we know each other from past lives?" Again, No. It turned out that Bob was just some random dead guy. He seemed more confused than we were. He definitely didn't hold the keys to unlocking the mysteries of the Universe.

At this point, Max was done. It had been a fun experiment, but he had better ways to spend his time. I understood his disillusionment with it all, yet I was undeterred by the lack of higher wisdom coming through. When Max left for work, I'd pull out the Ouija board and try it by myself. Of course, I'd watched enough horror flicks in my teenage years to be a little frightened to use this so-called toy on my own. Even though I wasn't sure if I believed in all the scary stuff, I took extra precautions by surrounding myself in a bubble of protective white light and always stating my intention that I only wished to connect to beings who serve love and light.

One day a being named Fanny came through. Fanny seemed to know a lot about Max. She provided a detailed explanation about the past life history between Max and his boss and how it was manifesting in their current issues at work. I was blown away by how much sense it all made, something I'd never considered. Fanny proceeded to scold me a bit for wearing the pants in my relationship with Max. She told me to give him more room to grow. Fanny was right and I took it in stride. She was tough but fair and also funny. She was obviously Max's spirit guide.

I couldn't wait to tell Max when he got home from work. Fanny was spot on, so Max couldn't help but be intrigued. We began daily sessions of connecting to Fanny through the Ouija board. Communicating through the board was a bit labor intensive and required patience as we watched each word spell itself out, letter by letter. At first I found myself sensing which letter would come next; then it developed to anticipating full words right before they spelled out on the board. Finally, whole sentences were coming in through my mind faster than our hands could move the pointer. It became much more efficient to simply speak the sentences I was hearing inwardly, while

Max would write it down. In this way, our sessions evolved so that we only used the board at the beginning to connect.

I loved Fanny's messages, but I couldn't help but feel a little disappointed. What about me? Where's my spirit guide? Soon enough, he showed up. He said his name was William, but asked us to call him Will. His energy was different from Fanny's. Will used a lot of puns, which I loved. He was playful, but also mysterious. Oftentimes, Will wouldn't give a clear answer to my many questions. Instead, he'd drop hints and have me "quest for the answer." Will said that despite how I think I want to know everything now, I'm actually the type who gets great joy from figuring things out on my own. So true!

Through Fanny and Will, a thrilling magical inner world opened up. It was as if unknowingly, I'd been experiencing the world in black and white, but now it changed to technicolor! I completely lost interest in the 3D world of work and mundane life. I lived for my time on the Ouija board.

One day, Will and Fanny said it was time for me to learn meditation. They explained that they resided in a higher vibration and they'd been dropping down their energy to match mine so that we could communicate. They had been acting as gatekeepers, blocking out other lower vibration beings who didn't have my best interests at heart. Ultimately, I needed to raise my vibration closer to their level. It would be ideal for our communication, plus it was necessary for my spiritual growth. Meditation was the way forward. They also said I needed to stop regularly using psychedelics, which were creating holes in my energetic field.

The psychedelics served their purpose of opening a door within me to expanded consciousness. Now that I had a source of higher wisdom through these guides, it was easy for me to let go of psychedelics. I didn't want them to be a crutch.

Meditation, on the other hand, was so challenging! When I'd sit and try to get quiet inside, frustration and restlessness would build up and torment me. It was anything but peaceful. Convinced that meditation wasn't for me, I gave up after several tries. It was easier just to go back to the Ouija board. It took merely seconds to connect. Why couldn't we just stick to what was working?

Not unlike loving but stern parents, Will and Fanny were adamant that I learn to meditate. They insisted that I keep practicing. They even limited our Ouija board sessions to just once every two weeks. I missed them so much, but I stubbornly refused to meditate. Why couldn't they see that meditation just wasn't my thing? One day they told me that they would no longer communicate using the Ouija board. I would have to practice meditation and learn to communicate with them inwardly.

I figured they must be bluffing. They wouldn't abandon me when we're just getting to know each other, right? I went to the Ouija board but nothing happened. No movement at all. I tried to use it on different days, different times. Nothing. I felt devastated. My vibrant multicolored reality became grey and dull again. The world of infinite possibilities and potential faded away.

I don't remember how much time passed, maybe days or weeks. Finally, I couldn't stand it. I missed the sense of aliveness, the love and the interconnectedness I felt when we used to communicate. I resolved to try as many meditation techniques as needed until something clicked. As I mentioned before, it would take almost a whole hour of listening to a guided meditation before I could get into what I now know is a higher vibrational state. But then I would just enjoy that deep state for another couple hours. I was deep into meditation one day when apparently Will spoke through my voice and instructed Max to grab a pen and paper. I began to channel verbally.

During these trance channeling sessions, I'd feel Will's energy and was vaguely aware he was speaking through me, but I couldn't remember anything he said. At first, Max was writing it all down, then he switched to a handheld recorder. We practiced over many weeks. In addition to Will, there were other non-physical beings that began showing up to help me channel: a loving motherly being named Anna and a group of three beings that seemed extraterrestrial. The group called themselves "We the Three" and their energy was impersonal but not cold.

The Three would sometimes show up in meditation and work on my chakras, especially the throat chakra, which is responsible for spirit communication. I'd feel wonderful after these sessions and the messages were enlightening, but I was a little disappointed that I couldn't communicate with them directly during trance channeling. Max was having a conversation with them. I would only learn what they communicated afterward.

Will said it would be better to develop conscious channeling, rather than trance channeling. In trance channeling, the spirit guide or being utilizes your body and communicates through your own voice while you're in a deep trancelike state. In conscious channeling, you stay in a lighter meditative state, raising your vibration so that you can simply tune into your spirit guide and have a conversation in your mind.

The benefit of trance channeling is that your mistrusting analytical part is subdued and out of the way. The drawback is not only the lack of conscious participation in the communication, but that it's also draining and possibly dangerous to bring other beings into your body if you're not careful. Conscious channeling is the overall better option, but the challenge is in learning to deal with the skeptical part of you that will inevitably be present, telling you you're making it all up.

It takes practice to be confident in conscious channeling, but it's well worth the effort. Healing the doubtful, fearful parts of yourself is a necessary step on the spiritual path. The only way forward is to face the discomfort. All growth follows the same process. It doesn't feel good at first to not know what you're doing. As you practice repeatedly, you acclimate to the process. You start to figure things out and improve. Finally, you get to a point where you feel at ease.

It's easy to get hooked on an unlimited supply of divine wisdom. Just remember, you're here on earth to learn through living your own experience. Just because you study something, doesn't mean you really know it. Just because spirit guides tell you something might happen, doesn't mean it will. We live in a free will universe. The way that you focus and the choices you make can shift the course from wherever you're heading to somewhere different. Working with loving spiritual beings can inform you, but you still need to take action in your life. Channeled information should leave you feeling better equipped to make your own decisions, rather than dependent upon spirit guides to tell you what to do.

I learned that lesson the hard way. There was a point in my life when I constantly checked with my guide Will for every little decision. Should I take this class? Should I apply here? One day he gave me a dose of tough love, telling me it was time to trust myself while he temporarily made himself scarce. Initially I felt abandoned. I'd read that some people ask their spirit guides for trivial things like help in finding a parking space. Mine won't even give me advice anymore?

Over time I came to realize that Will's actions were what I needed to grow. Without my guide to consult, I began to follow my own instincts again, which evolved through spiritual practices. More often my decisions were coming from my higher wisdom and less from fears or other people's influence. I needed that time away from Will to acknowledge my growth and to believe in myself.

My spirit guide eventually came back into the picture. He still comes and goes as he feels appropriate for my growth. I let go of those old codependent tendencies and now simply enjoy when he shows up. I know Will is always there, just dimmed in the background. The self reliance he cultivated empowered me with an unshakeable belief that in any challenging situation, I have what it takes to get through.

Here's a message from Will about Receiving Support from Your Spirit Guides:

*You are never truly alone. The human experience can be that of the illusion of separation. There is never a withholding of love or support from your guides or from spirit. It is your own ego that provides the experience of aloneness or separation. Fear, doubt, attachment, control and a myriad of other negative expressions that stem from the inability to be open to love block your awareness that you are always connected and supported.*

*You are aware of the metaphor of cutting open the cocoon to ease the struggle of the emerging butterfly, yes? This is the same concept. Although it pains us to see you struggle as you work through releasing your illusions, we recognize that we cannot hasten the process for you. We acknowledge that the struggle is a temporary and necessary stage in your transformation, providing you with the strength and motivation to break free into your true self, the higher expression of you.*

## Discernment When Working with Non-Physical Beings

You should always check the advice you receive from anyone, whether it's your father, best friend or your spiritual guide. Is it helpful? Does it make sense? Do you feel better after hearing it? Is the message positive and loving? Your spiritual development depends on the ability to discern your own truth. You need to learn to feel what resonates with you. Dismiss what doesn't resonate, regardless of the source of information. It's not necessarily wrong. It's simply someone else's truth.

We are all wise spiritual beings in our own right. Although it's become cliche, asking yourself, "What would Jesus/Buddha/Krishna (your favorite holy figure) do?" allows you to access your own higher awareness. When you imagine how to think or act as an enlightened being, you move into resonance with that higher vibration. Your thoughts and responses will come from a more evolved energy.

A high level spirit guide, similar to an excellent school teacher, will give you the opportunity to figure most things out on your own. They often choose to drop hints rather than give you a direct answer. They are supporting you in your development, not enabling a codependent relationship with them. My guide has often told me that he and my spiritual support team are cheering me on from the sidelines. Guides send love and encouragement as you face obstacles and celebrate your victories.

Be aware that there are many kinds of guides. They're not all at the same level of evolution. Your deceased grandmother may be loving and supportive, but she may not be more grown spiritually than your own higher self. It's necessary to develop your discernment when dealing with non-physical beings. Don't assume that because they are no longer in a body, they are an enlightened being. Do your due diligence when you connect with any non-physical being. Ask them if they serve love and light. If they don't answer, or if they say no, tell them to leave.

Here's some questions to ask yourself when connecting to a spirit guide:

- Does their energy feel loving?

- Am I uplifted during and after our connection?

- Do I feel judged by them or do they love me unconditionally?

- Are they offering guidance or are they telling me what to do?

- Do they make me feel pressured in any way?

- Do they help me to acknowledge my own gifts and inner knowing?

- Do their actions foster my independence or make me dependent on them?

High level spirit guides will never pressure you, nor make you feel as if you've disappointed them in any way. They know that time is just a construct of the 3rd dimension. Therefore you have as much time, as many lifetimes as you need to learn and grow. Yet being stuck in a pattern can be frustrating for you. It's empowering to finally get a lesson and move on. Your spirit guides will support you in opening to new perspectives, but will never do the inner work for you.

Generally, your guides or higher self will not divulge information that would interfere with your lessons. They may say things like "It's not appropriate for you to know that now." Try not to go to your spiritual support team to read your future. They aren't fortune tellers! You may think that you want to know your future, but in reality, it would take away all the fun if you knew what was going to happen next. Also, although you have some contracts with other souls for certain pre-agreed upon set events for your mutual growth, the majority of events are not set in stone. We are all co-creating each moment.

## Can Anyone Connect to Spirit?

Everyone can connect to spirit. Some people feel most comfortable communicating with their own divine consciousness. Regardless of how someone appears in their human form, each person has a wise and loving higher self. Others have a natural affinity with guides, angels or other higher beings. Who you choose to contact is only a matter of preference.

Spiritual beings never interfere with your free will. They encourage you to keep going as you struggle with life's challenges, but they won't step in unless your soul made that agreement with them prior to incarnating. If you didn't, it doesn't mean that you can't make such an agreement now. Sure, you drew up a blueprint for this life before you arrived, but your life choices created changes along the way.

If you sincerely desire to connect with higher consciousness for healing or growth, you won't be denied. This doesn't mean that all of your questions get answered or every wish is granted. They work with you according to what's aligned with your soul's purpose. Sometimes it's in your best interest to not be given answers, but to uncover them yourself.

It's a perfect process. People who have a lot of growing and maturing left to do usually aren't interested in focusing inwardly. They are drawn to outer world exploits of power, fame or maybe just survival. People who have learned these lessons in previous lives begin to look for answers within.

When you become interested in spiritual development, this interest naturally aligns you with the energies of your higher self and guides. They are always eager to assist those who seek help in growing themselves. Your guides and higher self live outside the veil of forgetfulness and the illusions of time and space. They see you in your true soul state. Much of their assistance is in guiding you to remember who you really are and to fulfill your unlimited potential.

Some of you are lucky enough to have personal cheerleaders like this in your physical life. Yet even those amazing people live within the constraints of earthly life and sometimes might not have the time and energy to help you. Your higher self and guides are always available to you with their unconditional love and wisdom. If they seem to be absent, they're probably hiding in the background, giving you room to grow. Their presence in your life is a true blessing.

Connecting regularly with higher beings grows you in another way: your energy frequency changes. Ever notice how when you hang out with optimistic people, you can leave feeling uplifted? It's similar to that. Each time you join with spiritual energy, you are reaching up to higher vibrations. Over time this gets easier and can become your natural state of awareness if you continue to think and act in alignment with this frequency.

Here's a message from Will on Inner Guidance:

*Inner guidance is a skill that is natural to some and takes time for others. It requires an equal measure of trust and patience with a dash of determination thrown in. One mustn't give up too easily, for the rewards greatly outweigh the time and effort required to develop this ability. Trust is the quality that is either the easiest or most difficult to come by, depending on the person. It is a precious gift to be able to trust oneself in any endeavor.*

*Once trust in one's inner self is established, few feats are unattainable. The world becomes alive with possibilities. Without inner trust, it is nearly impossible to attain lasting peace. Trusting others will continue to be a challenge as well. Trusting oneself requires nothing short of a leap of faith to get started. Once you begin to tune inside to your heart, you will be shocked and delighted at the wealth of wisdom seemingly contained in your heart.*

*Start small, simply acknowledging the little whispers of your inner voice. If you continue to honor those feelings and messages coming from your true self, greater mysteries will be revealed in time. Each of you carries far greater wisdom than you yet acknowledge. The process of uncovering your unique qualities and understanding is one to cherish. There are few greater joys than the unfolding of one's true self and the discovering of the source of light within. Everything in your life will be improved through development of the connection to your inner truth. The light within will naturally guide you to make more fulfilling, joyful, loving choices that honor your authentic self.*

# How to Connect With Your Higher Self or Spirit Guide

It's simple to work with the higher self and guides in self-hypnosis or meditation. Once you are in a relaxed, inner focused state, you just ask for them to appear. Your higher self will always show up when you call on it. It loves you so much that it gives you the free will to ignore it your whole life. But once you turn towards it and invite it in, it's so happy! Of course it will respond because it's been patiently waiting for the time when you'd be ready to work together with it. So trust that every time you reach for your higher self, it always responds. But it can take practice to trust your subtle inner senses and know that your higher self is there.

The way you experience your higher self varies. You have an inner version of all your outer senses: seeing, hearing, feeling, smelling, even tasting. Some people will see an image of a being or just light. It's common to feel love, joy or peace in their presence. You might also hear a voice or receive a message. Be open to all the ways they can reach out to you without expecting to experience it in a specific way.

Once you make that connection, first discern who they are by asking them if they serve love and light. Loving higher beings will always say yes. If there is no response or they say no, then tell them to leave. You have the power to choose who you allow into your energetic field. Once you have discerned that you are communicating with a loving being, you can ask for guidance on a particular issue. You can also request physical, mental, emotional or spiritual healing. Remember that they will provide whatever is appropriate for you to receive for your highest good at the time.

Your highest good doesn't always look the way you imagine it to be. From your limited 3D perspective, you may not be able to see how you are growing through a challenging situation. It might not be in your best interest to remove the situation, however, your guide or higher self can provide insight into what you're learning.

Not everyone feels a strong connection right away. Don't worry if what you feel is subtle at first. Each time you reach out for higher guidance, you are building a vibrational energetic bridge. With repeated practice, this bridge gets stronger, enabling you to connect more rapidly and receive messages more clearly.

Here's a message from Will on Channeling:

*There is always a message waiting to come through. So much inspiration and guidance is available and yours for the asking. Everyone has the ability to simply reach out and grab what they need to take the next step forward along their own path. Whether you decide to simply be open to whatever message greets you, or whether you prefer to focus* on a specific question is a matter of choice. Both methods work well for different purposes.

Recognize that you will always be drawing in guidance and support in your life. The determining factor of how much you can draw in is how open you are to receive. The next important factor is how clear you are inside. If you are clear and able to quiet yourself inside, you will best be able to decipher the messages. There are many who ask for guidance and yet are unable to recognize that they have already received it. It is like a wrapped present just waiting to be opened.

Unwrapping presents is a simple task. Even the youngest of children can rip open the packaging and discover what's inside. Sometimes, however, a person will unwrap the gift very carefully, making sure to savor the process and store the wrapping for later use. Either method works. Just recognize that the gift inside is the same, regardless of the method for unwrapping and regardless of the wrapping it comes in as well.

Sometimes the wrapping is what keeps you from even bothering to unwrap and look inside. Imagine that you have a pile of gifts with your name on it, all waiting to be opened. Some people automatically go for the biggest, most obvious gift to unwrap. Others dig in the pile for the smallest boxes, knowing they often hold the most valuable gifts.

When you're open to channel, you can ask for a particular gift or you can allow us to choose a gift for you. If you're sitting comfortably on the couch, eyes glued to the TV, you may never know that there's a pile of gifts waiting for you. When you open a gift, do you play with it, wear it, use it? Or do you just throw it aside and look for more gifts? Take time with each message you receive. These gifts have many uses and can be applied to many areas of your life. When you sincerely apply the *information you received, the next insight often comes automatically. When applied, it is self-generating.*

*The modern disposable way of life is not sustainable. Everything has such a short shelf life. Channeled guidance is a sustainable source of nourishment. When utilized, it keeps growing back even fuller, like the leaves of a basil plant. If you don't use it, the plant dries up and withers away. Things that circulate are healthy and sustainable. When money circulates, everyone can benefit from it. Your blood circulates to clear any impurities and keep you alive. Water that circulates is fresh. Channeled guidance must circulate also. Let it circulate into different areas of your life. Circulate the information by sharing it with others who can benefit. The circulation makes space for new ideas and information to be received.*

*Opening to receive, developing clarity, and circulating your gifts are simple ways to tap into your divine inner resources. Why not start now?*

## Get to Know Your Energy System

Quantum physics uncovered that nothing is solid; everything is energy. This means that every part of you is energy: body, mind, emotions, spirit. By learning to sense, feel and understand energy, you can know all the parts of yourself more clearly.

You carry your energy with you wherever you go. You are an energetic being. Everything that exists is a different frequency of energy. With practice, you can become aware of your energy all the time, paying attention to what you are radiating.

As you begin making energetic shifts through the inner practices you learn in this book, you'll notice that your outer world changes as you change. Your new vibration attracts people and opportunities of a similar vibration. Your energy also has the power to affect others and assist them in making their own shifts, if they are open to it.

Once you can sense energy, it becomes an indispensable tool for navigating your life. Energy doesn't lie. Appearances can be deceitful. Words can be untruths. But vibration cannot be faked. You cannot fake the vibration of love. You can't simultaneously embody the frequency of love and hate. When you sense love radiating from someone, you can know that their intentions are pure.

Sadly, I have met a few self-described healers whose vibration wasn't in alignment with their title. One was even highly praised by someone I respect. He had a spiritual look (whatever that means, ha ha) and the lingo down, but something just didn't feel right. I was surprised that I would energetically shut off in his presence, despite wanting to be my usual friendly and open self. Much later it was revealed that this man had cheated many people out of their money. As they say, "trust your vibes!"

I'm not suggesting that you only rely on energy to guide you. You are a multi-faceted being, with many important parts. Ideally, your ability to sense energy will work in conjunction with your physical senses, logic, heart and higher wisdom to lead you in life.

Working on the energetic level is incredibly powerful, due to the effect of resonance. Physics defines resonance as "a phenomenon in which an external force or a vibrating system forces another system around it to vibrate with greater amplitude at a specified frequency of operation." In plain English, that means that your vibration affects the energy of those nearby or those strongly connected to you.

We are all interconnected energetically, as if we are swimming in an invisible ocean of energy. Just by helping yourself feel better, you help others. While not everyone will accomplish big things on the world stage, you can positively affect others energetically through transforming your inner world. It may feel foreign at first, but it's in your interior reality where you have most control. Why not focus there first? In healing yourself, you become a more positive influence to those around you. Paraphrasing the popularly quoted but powerful words of Mahatma Gandhi, you become "the change you wish to see in the world."

In this section you'll learn about how to understand yourself utilizing the energy centers known as the chakras and an energy healing modality called Reiki. These are the energy systems I'm most familiar with, however, nowadays there are many energy modalities to explore and learn from. Choose whatever calls to you, just don't ignore working on the energetic level. It's the fastest way to transform spiritually.

Here's a message from Will on Embodying Spiritual Energy:

*You are radiating the light of your soul. Feel the empowerment of embodying this spiritual energy. Throughout the day, check back in briefly and reconnect and strengthen this energetic connection. The more you embody your own spiritual energy, the faster you manifest your highest intentions and dreams, which exist in the higher frequency energy.*

*It is your destiny and the destiny of all humans to eventually live as their own soul embodied in a human form. It is a process that begins very intentionally and requires continued focus, strengthening until it becomes your regular way of being. At first you cycle back and forth into the higher frequency. Don't be disappointed when you "come back down" to your regular vibrational resting point. This is natural and doesn't mean you are slipping. It is in fact the opposite. It requires consistent effort and patience to shift into a higher frequency.*

*Have compassion for where you're at and continue focusing your intention and behaviors to move you into a permanent shift in your energetic resting point. In this new higher frequency you will eventually discover that it becomes much easier to maintain behaviors that are aligned with your highest good and to let go of behaviors that no longer serve your growth.*

# Chakras

Chakras are your energy centers. There are seven main chakras in your subtle energy body that correspond to physical, mental, emotional and spiritual aspects of your being. Balanced chakras reflect a healthy body, mind and spirit. The chakras are a wonderful system you can utilize to see and understand yourself more deeply.

You can learn the qualities each energy center governs to get clarity on which parts of you need healing. For example, if you're someone who often loses your voice, you likely have throat chakra concerns to address. Or maybe you don't tend to have physical issues in the throat, but you're someone who has a hard time telling people no. This would still indicate throat chakra issues. The chakras are extremely useful in enabling you to be your own detective to pinpoint areas to focus on. As an energetic being, all aspects of your life are a reflection of the balance or imbalance of your own chakras.

Anything you want to create in the world starts off as a concept (crown chakra) and travels through your chakra system until manifestation in the physical world (root chakra). The clearer your chakras and energy body, the faster and easier it is to manifest what you want in your life.

The chakras are numbered starting from the slowest lowest vibration at the base of the spine to the highest fastest vibration at the crown of the head. Just as all of your body's organs are equally important, so are all of your chakras. They're a system, where each part has its own role in contributing to the overall balance and wellbeing of the whole. Each energy center can be balanced, underactive or overactive. Underactive means you need more energy there. Overactive means there is too much energy.

Let's do a brief overview of the primary seven chakras. While reading the descriptions that follow, you may get a sense of which chakras are needing your attention right now.

### 1st Chakra: Red - Base of Spine

Located at the base of the spine, this chakra governs your foundation, safety, survival, belonging, and the instinct to pro-create. Your most primal energies are located here. The energies of the base chakra (also known as root chakra) are earthy, supportive and stabilizing. This center houses the creative and primal energies of the kundalini. The element of this chakra is earth.

- Balanced: Feeling safe in the world, groundedness, physical body balance and connection, patience, emotional stability, prosperity and abundance, understanding of how to manifest in the physical.

- Overactive: Fearful, nervous, insecure, ungrounded, material-istic, greedy, resistant to change.

- Underactive: Lacking a sense of being at home or secure any-where, codependent, unable to get into one's body, fearful of abandonment, spaciness, experiencing lack and scarcity, in-security, fearful, flightiness, feelings of victimization.

### 2nd Chakra: Orange - Sacrum

Located just below the navel, it governs your emotional iden-tity, capacity for pleasure, desire, creativity, sexuality, intimacy and opens through the act of trust. The energies of this chakra are smooth, flowing, cool and soothing. The element associated with this chakra is water.

- Balanced: Self-esteem, pleasure, sense of deserving, healthy sexuality, creativity, playfulness, adaptability, spontaneity, vitality, abundance, receptive to change.

- Overactive: Overemotional, codependency, addictive personality, attracted to drama, moody, lacking personal boundaries, low self esteem, overindulgence in pleasure or sex, jealousy.

- Underactive: Stiff, unemotional, closed off to others, creative blocks, lacking self-worth, self critical, inauthentic, lack of desire, fatigued, a feeling of stagnation.

## 3rd Chakra: Yellow - Solar Plexus

This chakra sits within the solar plexus in the stomach area. It gives you a sense of who you are. It governs your will, decisiveness, intellect and personal power. You put your will into action through this chakra's energies. The element of fire fuels this chakra.

- Balanced: Sense of purpose, inner strength, having clear goals and motivation, feeling empowered, confident, self-disciplined, will power, productive, reliable, stable.

- Overactive: Domineering, aggressive, angry, perfectionistic. stubborn, judgmental, reactive, impatient.

- Underactive: Passive, indecisive, timid, lacking self-control, insecure, low self esteem, no will power, feeling lost with no sense of purpose, lack of energy/vitality, hesitant to act, help-lessness, fear of rejection.

4th Chakra: Green - Heart

This chakra is located in the center of the chest. It relates to issues of love, compassion, trust, and wellbeing. When it's activated, it stimulates a deep feeling of love or bliss. Blockages or imbalances can create a sense of depression or even hate. When this chakra is open, you treat yourself and others with kindness and respect. This chakra's element is air.

- Balanced: Emotional well-being, ability to give and receive unconditional love, compassionate, patient, open, joyful, able to forgive.

- Overactive: Loving in a clingy, suffocating way, lacking a sense of self in a relationship, willing to say yes to everything, lacking boundaries, over-giving, neglect of self care, code-pendent.

- Underactive: Cold, distant, lonely, unable or unwilling to open up to others, unforgiving, stubborn, negative, tense, feeling numb, overly critical, selfish, fearful, angry, lack of empathy, sense of disconnection, hopelessness.

5th Chakra: Sky Blue - Throat

Situated within the throat, the throat chakra is responsible for communication, expression and integrity. It reflects your authenticity, originality and truth. Sound is the element of this chakra.

- Balanced: Creative, speaking your truth, clear expression, authentic, good listener, living with integrity.

- Overactive: Overly talkative, unable to listen, highly critical, verbally abusive, gossipy, condescending.

- Underactive: Timid, insecure, fear of speaking up, unable to express needs, blocked creativity, biting your tongue, speaking softly, incoherent speech and communication, poor boundaries.

## 6th Chakra: Indigo - Forehead (Third Eye)

Directly within the center of the forehead, this chakra helps you channel and develop your ability to see spiritually. When the third eye is open it deepens your self reflection, awakens your intuition and gives you clear and pristine higher vision. It activates your inner senses such as clairvoyance, clairaudience, claircognizance and clairsentience. Light is the element for this chakra.

- Balanced: enhanced intuition and psychic abilities, imaginative, wise, integration of creativity and logic, self reflection, inspiration, clear thinking.

- Overactive: Out of touch with reality, lacking good judgment, unable to focus, mental fog, excessive daydreaming, prone to hallucinations.

- Underactive: Rigid thinking, closed off to new ideas, too reliant on authority, disconnected or distrustful of inner voice, anxious, clinging to the past and fearful of the future, lack of intuition, inability to perceive what's true, confused about your true purpose, unable to see the bigger picture.

### 7th Chakra: Violet - Crown

Sitting at the top of the head, this chakra opens the divine awareness of Oneness with all that exists. This is the connection to the soul. This chakra's element is thought.

- Balanced: Spiritually connected, able to see the beauty in all things, peace, reverence for life and nature, fair and ethical, transcendence.

- Overactive: Addicted to spirituality, apathy, neglectful of bodily needs, difficulty controlling emotions, superiority.

- Underactive: Not open to spirituality, unable to set or maintain goals, lacking direction, lonely, fearing death, overly intellectual, spiritual skepticism, materialistic, intolerant, unable to link the spiritual to physical.

Don't be discouraged if you notice that a number of your chakras are unbalanced. Your chakras are constantly fluctuating and have the potential to change almost as quickly as your mood, if you're open to letting go of old ways of being. There are numerous tools and techniques for healing your chakras and restoring energetic balance, everything from energy healing, aromatherapy, acupuncture, sound healing, yoga, color therapy, chakra meditation, and more.

Although I don't cover them here, there are additional 5th dimensional chakras activating now as we go through the Shift. I highly recommend that you take extra time to delve further into chakras. My favorite authors on this subject are Anodea Judith, Cyndi Dale and Ambika Wauters.

None of the chakras are better than the others. Each holds equal importance and must be proportional to one another. It's possible to open up some chakras much more than others and become imbalanced within yourself. Sometimes you need to focus on a particular chakra that is underdeveloped, in order to bring it into balance with the other chakras. Overall though, it's ideal to work with all seven chakras to maintain the proper energy harmony and foundation.

Excessive chakra work is a bit like playing with fire. There is a fiery primordial energy called Kundalini (the sleeping serpent) that can be awakened. Kundalini is the creative, evolutionary force of infinite wisdom that lives inside every single one of us. This is your latent, highest potential, so why should you be cautious about awakening it?

Once kundalini has begun awakening, it starts to move up your chakra system, clearing out whatever blockages it encounters. Kundalini's movement is unpredictable and the effects can be overwhelming to the unprepared. Kundalini has its own divine intelligence and works mostly outside of your control. Once activated, it's not possible to shut it down again, although you can somewhat mitigate its effects through lots of grounding and avoidance of any energetic or spiritual work. Kundalini is not to be feared, simply respected. As someone who has gone through a Dark Night of the Soul due to activated Kundalini, I would advise you to let it awaken in its own divine timing.

# Reiki

You might say I have a passionate love for Reiki that has only grown stronger after many years of practice.

Reiki is an energy healing modality that originated in Japan. Reiki came into my life shortly after I began meditating. Remember how I was meditating for three to four hours a day and bizarre stuff started happening? That's when I started feeling energy. As I was meditating, strange, new sensations would show up, particularly in my chakras. One moment I could feel giddy, almost high, and then the next I'd be crying, as sadness came up to clear. It was a fun but wild roller coaster ride of sensations and emotions.

I decided it would be wise to seek help from someone experienced in energy. A friend recommended I see a Reiki Master she knew, an older Japanese man who just happened to exactly fit a stereotype in my head. He was quiet and reserved, yet also loving and wise. His Reiki studio was so Zen: a simple room with a mat for me to lie on. He gave me Reiki in the traditional way, channeling energy through his hands while kneeling next to me on the floor.

Wow - I didn't know I could feel so good! After the session I inquired, "How can I feel like that all the time?" He suggested I learn Reiki. I didn't realize that anyone can learn Reiki, even kids. Reiki isn't restricted to special people born with healing hands, as I'd thought. It's available to anyone who sincerely wants it. Why wouldn't anyone want it? It feels amazing!

Not everyone starts off as sensitive to the energy as me, but everyone becomes more sensitive with more use. I eventually took all the classes and became a Reiki Master Teacher. One of the most surprising facts about Reiki is that it feels just as wonderful to give it as it does to receive it. Every time you give Reiki, you get filled with even more of this high vibrational energy.

I regularly tell my Reiki students that Reiki does everything and we do nothing. One of the best benefits of Reiki is that it's effortless. Once you get attuned to Reiki in a class, which means becoming opened as a channel for the energy, it works automatically through you simply with intention. Reiki is the healer, not you. You are the pure channel of the energy. You don't need to direct it. It naturally flows wherever it's needed. You don't need to figure anything out or know anything about the receiver. During a Reiki session, as the Reiki giver, you can just be present and enjoy experiencing the flow of energy through you to the receiver.

Being able to experience healing occurring through your Beingness, rather than your Doingness, is a lesson and a gift in itself. You've spent your life believing that nothing good will transpire without your effort. Due to this false belief, you've been constantly exerting yourself to make things happen, not realizing you're on a never-ending hamster wheel. This way of life is unsustainable. It takes its toll on your body, showing up as mystery symptoms or illnesses.

At first it's so hard to believe that healing is happening when you, the Reiki practitioner, are doing nothing! It's a bit magical. After you've experienced it enough times, you're able to fully relax and trust Reiki. You realize that we are all part of a bigger stream of energy. When you open to that greater current of high frequency energy, it can gently wash away whatever is stuck, whatever you're ready to let go of. Reiki restores your energetic flow.

Let go of the idea of wanting "good energy" and releasing "bad energy," and instead, just focus on flow. Qualifying energy as good or bad gets us stuck in unnecessary judgment. Everything is simply energy. Everything that's healthy flows. Money is meant to flow freely in a healthy economy; that's why it's called currency. If people are worried and no one spends their money, we have a bad economy. The fluids in your body need to circulate. When your fluids get blocked, you get sick. Once stagnant energy begins to move again, health restores. Flow is the key to your wellbeing.

As I mentioned, at first I learned Reiki just because I wanted to feel good. There's absolutely nothing wrong with wanting to feel good if it doesn't harm others, which Reiki certainly doesn't. Yet my relationship with Reiki evolved over time. It's deceptively gentle. Don't let that fool you into thinking it's not powerful. Comfortably, organically, I've completely transformed over time, largely due to a combination of Reiki and meditation.

These two practices steadily wash away all the crud you've accumulated that doesn't serve you: painful emotions, limiting beliefs, fears, unhealthy patterns. For me it happened so gradually that it became normal to feel unfettered and free. One day I was shocked when someone's neurotic energy flashed me back to my old mindset. I'd simply forgotten I was ever like that! When exactly did that change? I tried unsuccessfully to pinpoint when the shift occurred, but there wasn't one specific moment. Realizing that change can happen comfortably, even joyfully, is another blessing bestowed by these practices.

To get started with Reiki, you'll need to take a class. Nowadays Reiki classes are accessible to everyone. Don't despair if you can't find a local Reiki Master teacher. Many teachers, like myself, offer online Reiki classes. Energy is not constrained by time or space.

While Reiki has endless benefits, I'll leave that for another book. If I could only recommend one practice for your spiritual journey from this entire book, I would choose Reiki. Why? Because Reiki is a "jack of all trades." Some tools heal your physical body. Others help your mind or emotions. Still others provide spiritual benefits. Reiki can be applied for any of these areas, because body, mind and spirit are all energy at different frequencies. Anyone who regularly practices Reiki cannot help but raise their vibration over time.

# Reflect: Journal

*"The unexamined life is not worth living." -Socrates*

I sometimes joke that if my home were on fire, I'd run into the flames to save my journals. Why? They contain this life's saga, every obstacle, hope, mystery, sorrow, victory, despair, awakening, and so much more. All those pages of hard-earned insights are not just badges of honor; they're reference books that I regularly consult to provide deeper understanding of what's happening in my life now.

It's often only in the greater context of your entire life story that your current challenges make sense.

There's no one "proper" way to journal. I prefer the tactile experience of using a fine point pen to write on lined paper. I love shopping for a new journal, selecting a gorgeous book that inspires me to keep my deepest thoughts tucked away between its covers. You might prefer the speed of typing on your laptop and having the ability to categorize and quickly search through your entries for a particular topic. You can even create audio or video journal entries if you'd like.

Regardless of the medium, a journal is an invaluable resource for chronicling your spiritual journey. You know the expression, "Hindsight is 20/20," right? That's because when you're deep in the middle of a situation, it can be challenging to rise above and see it from a higher point of view. Emotions and subconscious beliefs get triggered, clouding your perspective. Often, you need time to sit with your experience and work through it. Journaling is an excellent method for processing your thoughts and feelings, bringing you new insight.

If you're too busy to stop and reflect from time to time, you'll find that you are living a mostly reactive life. You may feel like a victim to outer life events. "Why is this happening to me? It's not fair." It's useful to remember that everything is energy and interconnected. Whatever shows up in your life is aligned with something in your energy, even if you can't see it yet. Rather, your energy is attracting circumstances to you to teach you something, yet you're missing the gift it offers.

When I'm going through a tough time I go back through my journal and see all of the joyous experiences. It helps me put things into perspective and remember those immortal words, "This too shall pass."

# Explore Your Dreams

*"The dream is a little hidden door in the innermost and most secret recesses of the soul, opening into the cosmic night which was psyche long before there was any ego-consciousness, and which will remain psyche no matter how far our ego-consciousness extends." -Carl Jung*

Perhaps you feel you have little time to read chakra books, practice channeling or take Reiki classes. You're still struggling with meditation. Yet you have a strong desire to know your Self deeply, to uncover the obstacles that stand in the way of your fulfillment. Then why not explore dreamwork?

Dreams are a fascinating tool for examining your own psyche, through bypassing your critical conscious mind to discover hidden treasures in your subconscious and superconscious minds. During the day you may be blocking the subtle inner feelings from your emotions and intuition and instead favor your logical conscious mind. In this way you can accomplish a lot, yet have a nagging feeling that something you can't seem to place is missing. You're overlooking important keys to self awareness and growth.

A dream is a built-in portal to the inner realms. Dreams contain a treasure chest of insights. The meaning of each dream can be unraveled through intuition and analysis. If you're seeking personal growth and healing, dreams are excellent indicators of what needs attention.

Without the restriction of the analytical mind blocking it, all that you haven't been willing or able to face can come up through dreams. This is a gift! Dreams are the pathway to the deep wisdom buried under all the daily activities. Don't disregard dreams as nonsensical. They simply speak to you in a different language than you're used to, through abstract sensory expression, much like art.

Similar to art, you understand a dream's meaning by how it makes you feel. Your feelings are the clues to the insights hidden in a dream. As you focus on the emotions evoked through the dream, contemplate on if that resonates with your everyday life. Perhaps in your dream you were trapped in a cave. In what area of your life do you feel trapped? Have you been ignoring that feeling, telling yourself it's not so bad? What wisdom is your dream pointing you to realize?

Some people struggle with interpreting their dreams. In meditation or with hypnosis, you can tap into the energy of a dream and interact directly with the symbols to unlock their meanings. In this relaxed inner-focused state, you can re-enter the dream to either continue the story to a satisfactory conclusion or to talk to the characters and learn what they represent. Continuing the story is a fun and easy way to shift the energy of an issue, without necessarily even knowing what the issue is. You become responsible for the storyline and empowered to make necessary changes. Changes first made inwardly are then reflected in the outer world. In this case, you do the work which creates the shift and the insights come later.

Interacting with the symbols and characters of the dream produces the insight first. Once you go back into the dream, approach someone and ask questions like: Who are you? Why are you here? What do you want from me? What do you represent?

This works even with inanimate objects. Just imagine you have telepathic abilities. You can tune into the object and begin asking questions. What do you symbolize? Why are you in my dream? What message do you have for me?

Dreams are a wellspring of self knowledge, which can propel your spiritual development. They happen automatically every night. Why waste this precious resource?

Although my waking life memory is subpar, I've been blessed with vivid dream recall since I was a child. Certain dreams have impacted me even more deeply than outer life events, providing soul nourishment and inspiration at the most challenging points of my life.

My own experiences have led me to believe that our soul travels out of body every night when we sleep. Years ago I had a series of similar transportation dreams several nights in a row. In the first dream, I'm on a motorcycle, riding at high speeds along a dirt road, feeling free. Suddenly, the motorcycle begins shaking uncontrollably. Fear washes over me and then moments later, everything smooths out and I'm calm. The next night I dreamt of being on a speedboat and the same thing happened. The third night I was on a train. After this dream, I took note of the pattern and the specific feeling it evoked every night. Before going to bed I told myself, 'Next time I find myself traveling at high speeds and then feeling out of control, I'll know I'm dreaming!'

Sure enough, I'm going up in a helicopter when it begins to wobble violently. As the fear emerges, I realize I must be dreaming. The moment I become lucid, the dream landscape fades. I find myself floating above my body, which is asleep in bed! It dawns on me that the shaking I experienced in the dreams is what's known as the vibrational state in astral projection. In this state, it feels like your whole body is shaking violently. It occurs just before you release from the physical body. My consciousness had been creating a dream story to explain that sensation every night while I exited my body during sleep.

Many indigenous cultures, as well as some religions, and also other people who are experienced in astral projection, such as author Robert Monroe, came to the same conclusion. Astral projection is another fascinating tool for exploring different realms of consciousness. Conscious out-of-body travel requires dedicated practice, but if you have the patience, it's well worth the effort. There are many excellent guides on the subject, including books by Robert Monroe, William L. Buhlman, Robert Peterson, Robert Bruce (why so many Roberts?) and more.

Back to dreams! There are many types. In the most common type of dream, you work on the subconscious "lower self" level, processing emotions and becoming aware of limiting beliefs. These dreams can seem ordinary, like scenes out of your everyday life. Nonetheless, they're valuable in showing you what you're not seeing because you've been too busy to notice. In a superconscious dream, you explore the higher spiritual realms, receiving wisdom from your spirit guides, visiting deceased loved ones and even doing valuable healing work for yourself and others. These dreams often feel magical, imbued with loving energy, vivid colors or beautiful ethereal music. You wake up inspired and energized to face the day.

Because time is only a construct in our 3D reality, when you travel out of body during sleep into higher dimensions, you can experience past lives, parallel lives or the future. As you continue to raise your vibration through your spiritual practices, you will likely find yourself naturally tapping into more of these non-ordinary type dreams. Also, the more you honor your dreams by paying attention to them and recording them, the greater the likelihood that your dream practice will progress and you'll also remember more.

You might be one of those who think you don't dream. Scientific research shows that we all dream. So it's just a matter of improving your recollection. The easiest way is to keep a pen and notebook by the bed to record your dreams. Don't get out of bed when you first wake up. Instead, grab the pen and notebook and write down any impressions from the night, even if it's just a feeling or one image. If you don't remember anything, write down "I don't remember anything." Oftentimes you'll find that as you're writing, some dream information emerges. By simply making the effort to write even the smallest dream bit every morning, you are signaling to your consciousness that this is important to you. You can train yourself to remember your dreams by building the dream memory muscle with diligence over time.

Happy dreaming!

# Discover Your Past Lives

As you begin to explore inwardly through meditation, journaling and dreamwork, your self awareness grows. You realize there is much more to you than even realized. Memories may awaken of other versions of you in other times and places.

I first touched into a past life during meditation. Back in the early days of my spiritual journey, when I was meditating for long periods at a time, all sorts of unusual things began to happen. At that point, I still lacked a greater understanding of the process of evolution through reincarnation. In fact, I wasn't sure that I even believed in the concept, but I was open to whatever Spirit wanted to show me.

Imagine my surprise when after an hour of quieting my mind and getting into a deeper state, I suddenly found myself in a different body in a different place and time! I didn't see these other lifetimes clearly, the way I do this one. But the feelings of being these other people was intense. There was one week where every single day when I meditated, I would end up in a past life. I was a man, a child, an elderly person. I experienced being different ethnicities and every kind of person imaginable - rich, poor, kind, cruel.

There's no way I could make up having the awareness of being someone else. It's intimate and sometimes shocking to experience firsthand another person's thoughts and perspective, which are at times radically different from your current life. You have dual awareness of the current you and the past life you throughout the regression. Even though these two perspectives may contrast greatly, there's an understanding that you are both of these and yet are also the greater consciousness beyond these limitations.

Sometimes people ask, "Why bother focusing on your past lives? Shouldn't we just stay focused on the present?" Revisiting past lives is not something you do just for fun or curiosity. It always helps you in some way in your current life, whether that's through clearing out karma, gaining new insight or simply in remembering forgotten parts of yourself.

Past life regression is one of countless methods to heal and grow yourself. Recognizing that there are many paths up the mountain, always choose methods that you feel drawn to. You are most likely to stick to a path you enjoy. Not every past life is exciting. In fact, past lives can be mundane or traumatic. Yet, people derive pleasure from experiencing life in an alternate time and place, in another body.

Being able to experience the world from an entirely different viewpoint is liberating, a vacation from being yourself without a hangover. This other perspective remains with you after the session. If you were confident and strong, you can tap into that mindset whenever you need it because you remember what it's like. If you were also rude and arrogant, you might now avoid that tendency in this life because you recall the repercussions of your actions. Or you may even be able to find compassion for rude, arrogant people by remembering how it felt to be one. Like everything else in life, the benefits derived from past life regression depends on your intent. This shift in awareness and focus is a major growth opportunity. No longer do you perceive the world only from the narrow viewpoint of your current life experiences.

There's an expression: Before you judge a person, walk a mile in their shoes. Through past life regression, you recognize the diversity of shoes you've walked in. Your capacity to comprehend different ways of being is no longer simply intellectual, it's now experiential. You understand how life experiences impact the beliefs and characteristics of a person. Through this expanded perception, you can release judgment of yourself and others.

You might not be sure if you believe in reincarnation as I do, however, how will you know if you haven't fully explored the possibility? Through my experiences I came to understand that we incarnate as humans for the awareness we gain by learning lessons through physical experience. Perhaps nothing is impossible, but it's highly unlikely that a soul can learn all of its lessons in one lifetime. So we return again and again until we've learned all that's available.

There are so many possible areas to study: forgiveness, humility, self expression, empowerment, unconditional love, etc. In your soul state, you are all of these things. To truly know these aspects of yourself, you choose to incarnate and forget the totality that you are - to experience the joy of rediscovering each aspect of self.

Just like in school, some areas of study continue across several lifetimes. For instance in math, you need to take Algebra 1 before taking Algebra 2. Other areas are unrelated to each other. You could take Algebra 1 one semester and then no math the next semester. You could spend one life in challenging personal relationships, focusing on learning forgiveness. The next life's lesson may be unrelated, spent in solitude, developing a craft and learning perseverance. In a later life, you may pick up from where you left off in the lesson of forgiveness. It's not necessarily a linear process, however you never lose whatever awareness you've gained in your physical lives.

It's not important that you remember all of your past lifetimes. At this point in your soul's evolution, many of them are already processed, healed and integrated. Although the fact that you're currently incarnated means that most likely you do still have some karma left to clear, you can also trust that it tends to come up when you're ready for it. When I first awakened to spirituality, I spontaneously went into many past life experiences during meditation. Then there were several years when I didn't feel drawn to explore past lives and nothing came up during meditation. When I eventually felt called to study hypnosis, I began experiencing them again. Have faith that the right experiences and opportunities show up in your life when you are an energetic match for them.

# CHAPTER 3

# Love Yourself

There are few people alive who haven't been told at some point, "Love yourself." Almost everyone would agree that it's a good thing to love yourself. Why is it such a challenge for most of us? Earthly love tends to be conditional. When you declare your love, you might not even be aware that there's an unspoken "I love you on the condition that..."(you love me back, you give me what I need, you behave appropriately, etc.) That's true not only for the way you love others, but also for how you love yourself.

Love is the building block of the spiritual existence. True love seems so hard to find here in the 3rd Dimension because there's the illusion of separation from Spirit, which is the source of pure love. Although your soul chose this illusion intentionally for your growth, your 3D self may experience a disconnection from Source, feeling abandoned. You've forgotten that you wanted to find your way back to Spirit through your own free will. Think of a child who is born "with a silver spoon in their mouth" but chooses not to take their mom and dad's money because they want to develop the ability to earn it themselves. Substitute love for money and you'll get the idea spiritually.

If you remembered from the start that no matter what you do here on Earth, you're always safe and loved, you might not take this experience seriously. The obstacles wouldn't seem real, therefore you wouldn't grow the way you needed to overcome them. The illusion of feeling incomplete has driven you to challenge yourself, move out of your comfort zone and persevere. It drove you to find answers and through that quest you discovered Spirit.

When you rediscover Spirit, you undoubtedly encounter love. True love. Pure unconditional love, which asks for nothing and gives endlessly. By plugging into this infinite source of love, your capacity to love yourself and others transforms. Everyone knows, "You have to fill your own cup first before you have something to give others." People try to fill their cup up with love from other people, but inevitably are disappointed.

You are certainly loved by other people, but the love they have to share is limited by their capacity to love themselves and whether they're filled up from within first. Those who receive love from the infinite source may be overflowing with love to share. Others are giving from their limited supply and therefore unconsciously need and expect you give the same back to fill them up again. This is the conditional love that most people on Earth experience.

As you drink from the fountain of Divine Love, you awaken to the reality that love is not found outside of you. Your true essence is love. Love is the most powerful healer that exists. You begin to shine the light of love into all the dark corners of your Being, the places in which you denied love because you deemed them ugly, shameful, not good enough.

It's not enough to realize you are divine and to then focus on your higher self. To become your higher self, you must love and accept your lower self as well. You are one being comprised of many parts: body, spirit and a personality that consists of many sub-personality parts. This section addresses aspects that you almost always need to reclaim and nurture. Included are practices for loving and integrating these lower parts, which will bring you into a state of wholeness.

Here's a message from Will on Self Love:

*Finding in your own heart that which you are seeking to receive will bring you to deep fulfillment and naturally attract more to you. You are not lacking or empty. You have much to give. Dip into the well of love and affection buried in your own heart and drink from it first. Drink until you feel refreshed and satisfied. Then you may begin pouring some out to share with others.*

*Looking at yourself with love and acceptance makes it easier to do so with others. Start small. Find one thing each day to appreciate about yourself. Keep adding to the list. When it becomes second nature, you will undoubtedly notice you have drawn in more love and joy into your life. Start today and enjoy the path of nurturing love in your own heart.*

# Parts Integration

You tend to think of yourself as a single unit. This is true of course, but you are also a multi-faceted being, made up of varied aspects of self.

Our societal preoccupation with competition and being a winner creates intense self judgment and separation of your aspects. You learn to label some parts of yourself as good and others as bad. You're taught to "Be strong. Highlight strengths. Eliminate weakness." This approach may be effective for becoming a better competitor, but at what cost to your wellbeing?

Shame, judgment, self loathing, fear of failure, unhappiness, disconnection and the inability to nurture yourself are some of the effects of this win/lose approach to life. You want to show off your "good" qualities and hide or suppress your "bad" qualities. You think others will like you more this way, yet you feel like a fraud, afraid of your unacceptable parts getting discovered. Because of this, you may keep people at a comfortable distance, yet part of you yearns to connect more deeply and authentically. This separation exists not only with others, but within yourself. Ironically, by cutting yourself off from the "bad" parts, you diminish your life force and reduce your capacity to develop into your highest potentiality.

Self esteem based upon success and outer gratification is precarious and exhausting. You are stuck in the endless race of trying to prove your worth to yourself and others through your accomplishments. You are drained trying to control outer circumstances to ensure your success. The way out of this trap is through self love and compassion.

Clients sometimes ask me to assist them in getting rid of their "bad" parts using hypnosis. Here's what I tell them:

*All of your parts are good. A lot of them were established during childhood when you had less resources and wisdom to develop them. They got labeled as bad and you locked them away in the deep inner recesses of your being where they never received any nourishment. Then they got beaten down with judgment and criticism. How can they get better that way?*

*Everything grows with love. Imagine having two bosses. One always cuts you down. Despite your best efforts, nothing is ever good enough for them. The other one is very supportive. When you make a mistake, they show you how you can improve in an encouraging way. Who are you going to work harder for? Of course, the supportive one. In fact, they build up your energy, whereas the other one diminishes you and you become less effective.*

You don't realize that self criticism doesn't make you better. It weakens you. Self compassion doesn't mean pretending like you did a good job when you made a mistake. It means changing your inner dialogue from, "You're such an idiot! You're never going to get it right!" to something like, "Ok, let me figure out what I did wrong and fix it. Everyone makes mistakes. The important thing is to learn from them."

With the right inner nourishment, all of your parts can develop into their highest potential. The embarrassing awkwardness becomes a quirky charm. The overzealousness matures into a passion for life. The nitpicking transforms into thoughtful attention to detail.

The process of healing and growth requires that you not only nourish and accept your parts, but also harmonize them. These parts, called sub-personalities, have developed at different times in your life in response to the beliefs you were raised with and to your life experiences. One part of you may crave adventure, while another part needs security. One part may love interaction, while another part prefers seclusion. The dynamic amongst the particular aspects can create inner conflict.

Keep in mind that many of your sub-personalities formed at a young age. By ignoring them, you haven't allowed these parts to mature alongside your intellect or spiritual awareness. You needn't be ashamed of this disparity. It's not uncommon for the intellectual self to be more developed than the emotional self, because our society highly prizes the intellect and tends to place less value on feelings. Yet you need all parts to complete the whole.

It's important to bring these different aspects together under a common goal. Think of it like a team. Each team member has their own personality which may clash with the others. A great coach unites the team through their leadership. Up until now, your ego was likely trying to control the team. Your soul needs to be the leader.

Only your soul, with its higher awareness, love and acceptance can be entrusted to make wise empowered choices that serve the good of all your parts. With your soul leading the pack, the common goal becomes elevated to "your highest good." When spiritual growth becomes your goal, you shift focus from societal values to inner truth. Allowing your soul to lead will free you and bring you into alignment with your true self.

Anytime you feel stuck in life, it's because two or more aspects of yourself are pushing against each other. You can use the Parts Integration Technique to create a new approach that honors and balances the needs of each part so that you can move forward.

## PARTS INTEGRATION TECHNIQUE

1. Begin with meditation, self hypnosis or simply by getting quiet and directing your attention inside yourself.

2. Inwardly call on your soul to connect with you more deeply. Your soul always wants to connect more with you, however, it respects your free will. Therefore, when you call on your soul, it always shows up for you. Trust this, even if you aren't sure if you can sense or feel your soul's presence yet.

3. Imagine placing the part of you that doesn't want to move forward in one hand and the part of you that wants to move forward in the other hand. It doesn't matter which hand which represents which part. Understand that each part is a valid part of you trying to get its needs met through its behavior. It's important that you don't label one part as good and the other as bad.

4. Now give one part the opportunity to express itself without interruption from the other side. What is important to it? What is it afraid of? What does it need right now?

5. Switch sides and ask the other part the same questions.

6. Each part can see that the other part isn't bad, just different. Now you, with the guidance of your soul, can mediate the discussion between the two until an agreement is made for a small step moving forward that meets the needs of both.

7. You may need to do this process of meditation many times for these parts until they learn how to work together. It gets easier with practice.

In the next two sections, Shadow Work and Inner Child Healing, we'll look at two often overlooked and undervalued parts of your psyche. Reclaiming these parts is a major key to being able to love yourself.

# Shadow Work

The process of spiritual awakening is ultimately a process of becoming balanced and whole. Oftentimes it seems like what you want is just out of your grasp. What if the answer was right under your nose? What if your greatest gifts were right below the surface, the ones you couldn't see? This is the power of the shadow.

What exactly is the shadow? Carl Jung defined the shadow as "everything a person refuses to acknowledge about himself." Although everyone has a shadow, it is obviously different for each person and varies greatly with the values and culture you are raised in. Jung believed that the shadow is the seat of your creativity.

In the Parts Integration section, we covered how you were taught to separate and label parts as good and bad, acceptable and unacceptable. The acceptable parts remain in your conscious awareness. The unacceptable parts comprise the shadow and become hidden. Determined not to show these parts to others, you either spend a lot of energy keeping them hidden or you forget you have them entirely and instead project them onto others.

In Debbie Ford's excellent book, "The Dark Side of the Lightchasers," she explains that ignoring a part doesn't make it go away. Rejecting a part of yourself usually makes it even stronger. People spend their whole life struggling to control some aspect of themselves.

Perhaps you can remember a time when your feelings seemed way out of proportion to the situation. Your emotion got triggered and the feeling just took over. Afterward you thought to yourself, "That's so unlike me. Why was my response so over the top?" This is a common scenario of the shadow acting out. Like a wayward teenager, it forces you to pay attention to it. You can't bottle it up forever.

The energy used to hold this shadow down creates a pressure cooker inside. Your fear gives this shadow strength and power over you. You are no longer free. You act carefully to not expose this ugly part to the world. In fact, trying to suppress it has the opposite effect. Pushing down against this part actually strengthens it. It grows bigger and becomes distorted in the process. At some point the pressure becomes so strong that it bursts out uncontrollably. You then feel ashamed and vow to push it down further, repeating the cycle.

What you resist, persists. If the shadow has become totally hidden and unconscious, you'll find yourself attracting whomever you need to mirror back your disowned aspects. Although you've hidden your shadow, you carry its energy within and it magnetically draws people with matching energy into your life. These people will often be an amplified version of your disowned quality, which makes the quality impossible to miss but difficult to accept. If you want to stop drawing these unpleasant people into your life, you need to own that quality within yourself.

Perhaps as a child you cried at night, afraid of the boogeyman in the closet. Your mom or dad came into your room and turned on the light to reassure you that it was safe. As an adult what you don't realize is that the bogeyman you're so frightened of is just a neglected part of yourself. You can shine the light of awareness onto these shadow parts and watch them transform before your eyes.

In each part of yourself that you have overlooked or disowned, there's always a gift hidden beneath the dark exterior. With shyness, there may be the gift of introspection. With anger, there may be the gift of strength or passion. Just recovering all the energy used to conceal the shadow is a gift in itself. Releasing the fear of identifying with this "bad" part diffuses its energy so that it no longer controls you. Now you can better manage this aspect and use it in appropriate situations. By summoning the courage to face each of these parts, you become stronger and more confident.

One of the greatest gifts of reclaiming your shadow is freedom from judgment of self and others. You recognize your vulnerability as well as your strength. You see your naïveté as well as your wisdom. You realize you have the capacity to be any quality in addition to its total opposite. This awareness awakens compassion and releases judgement, both within and without.

My initial introduction to Spirit was of the "love and light" variety: wise spirit guides, thrilling adventures out-of-body in the Cosmos, activation of intuitive gifts, magical realizations and waves of love. It was straight out of a fantasy novel. And while all of that is valid and just as possible for you and everyone else, it's essential to realize that soul embodiment requires acceptance of the light and dark. In fact, for many people, spiritual awakening is a by-product of the darkest point in their life: a tragedy, loss or hitting rock bottom in some way.

It doesn't matter if you initially open to Spirit through the light or the dark, eventually you'll need to face your shadow on the journey, otherwise you'll end up spiritual bypassing. Psychologist John Welwood coined the term "spiritual bypassing." He said, "When we are spiritually bypassing, we often use the goal of awakening or liberation to rationalize what I call premature transcendence: trying to rise above the raw and messy side of our humanness before we have fully faced and made peace with it." It's an ego defense mechanism to escape the discomfort of the human emotions under the pretense of having moved beyond it spiritually.

Beware that the ego loves to operate under the cloak of spirituality. What better hiding place for all of the appalling humanness than behind an idealized persona of an evolved spiritual being, deluding yourself that you have mastered your thoughts and emotions? I went through this phase myself, at the beginning of my spiritual path. I was receiving incredible insights, having paranormal experiences, feeling unimaginable bliss and hearing messages from spiritual guides. It was easy for my ego to latch onto this idea that I'd evolved spiritually and transcended lower human emotions and desires. I would look at the world with disdain, wondering why everyone else didn't get it and chose to remain in their lower selves.

I was stuck in this stage for at least a year. Eventually, I had a few scary run-ins with a shadowy figure while astral projecting. Every time I'd travel out-of-body, it would chase me and try to bite me. It began interfering with communications with my spirit guide Will, threatening me and calling me names. It frightened me so much that I began to question the whole spiritual journey. How did I know for sure who I was talking to when I channeled? What if a dark force had been tricking me this whole time?

I stopped all spiritual practices for months and tried to go back to ordinary life. Everything became grey again. The numbness set in. I didn't want to go back to the business world, but without spirituality, I didn't see a path forward. The meaninglessness of life weighed heavily on me.

It was at this point that unexpectedly (although now I know it was guided by Spirit) I found a wonderful spiritual school called Delphi University and began to take classes there. I learned the value and importance of the lower chakras and realized that I'd been spiritually bypassing. I was only focusing on the upper spiritual chakras and had overlooked the necessary mental and emotional foundational work in the lower chakras. All of my hidden unhealed lower energy manifested or attracted similar energy, this shadowy figure, when I was in the astral realm. This also commonly happens in the physical world: you attract an outer representation of your own repressed energy.

This is a common stage on the spiritual path. There's nothing to be ashamed of if you're going through this, but it's important to recognize it and shift out of it. Shadow work will help you transform. Once you recognize that anything you're judging outside of you is a reflection of something you can't accept within you, the way out is through compassion. Remember that we are all pieces of the Oneness going through different stages on the path.

This spiritual bypassing dynamic is prevalent amongst the "Good Vibes Only" tribe, who mistakenly believe that rejecting negativity is the path to spiritual evolution. Negating the darkness doesn't bring you into wholeness. Your ego is not going to disappear now that you are on a spiritual path. You need an ego to survive as a human being. You just have to keep it in check and not allow it to run the show. In fact, by acknowledging your ego's existence, you'll be able to gently guide it.

## HOW TO ACCESS THE POWER OF YOUR SHADOW

As a certified clinical hypnotist, I have clients coming to me because they want to change or heal some aspect of themselves. Oftentimes people think the solution they're looking for is to get rid of a part that is unacceptable. In fact, the solution is the complete opposite. Just like in physics, this energy cannot be created or destroyed. Underneath the unacceptable behavior is a valid need. While in hypnosis you access the part that is creating the behavior, for example smoking or getting stage fright. Once you address this part and discover its needs, you can come up with new positive behaviors to meet those needs. That part that was once disenfranchised can now be integrated.

Despite the fact that you've hidden it, the shadow is easy to uncover once you are willing to face it. To get started, here's a couple of simple exercises from the book "The Dark side of the Lightchasers" by Debbie Ford:

- Begin by listing all the people who really get under your skin. This may be people you know personally as well as public figures. Notice what specific traits of each person bother you. With each trait on the list, think of a time when you behaved the same way or think of a situation in which you would be capable of feeling the same way. Sometimes you will need to break it down to the base underlying emotion. For instance, you may not feel capable of murder, however you can think of a time when you were enraged or when you hurt another with your words.

- Make a list of all the parts you don't like and find at least one gift hidden in each part. For example, if you were raised believing that people should be humble, your shadow may be a showoff. Gifts of being a showoff may be not being afraid to speak up, or the ability to demonstrate self-confidence. If you have difficulty finding the gift in a particular trait, ask a friend to help. Each person has their own unique blinders.

The point isn't to become the opposite of who you are or what you value. You don't have to fall in love with all of your parts, just own them and see their value. By recognizing you are also the opposite of what you identify with, you become balanced. In recognizing you are every trait, you become whole. When you are balanced and whole, you become free to choose how you want to be in each moment and act with awareness.

Confronting the darkness within gives you empowerment. If you act as if your own feelings aren't important, how can you expect anyone else to value them? By no longer running from any part of yourself, you're telling yourself that you matter.

How can you face dark emotions when they seem overwhelming? First, let go of the notion that you need to fix emotions. Resist the urge to try to solve whatever situation triggered the emotion. Simply sitting with the emotion and experiencing the sensation in the body allows it to begin processing.

Second, notice if the feeling wants to express. If so, allow it to flow, whether through tears, a sigh or scream, or through writing or movement. Finally, send love to the part of you that's hurting - whether it's from sadness, anger, fear or any other dark feeling. Love is the most powerful healer.

Honoring all of your feelings in this way releases them or lessens their intensity. Often what you fear outwardly is a reflection of your own darkness. You build your walls but it never gives you a sense of security because you haven't addressed the true source, your own shadow self. As you begin to face the inner darkness, you allow light to enter, the light of inner peace.

Here's a message from Will on Healing the Shadow:

*You must heal the disowned shadow parts of yourself that sabotage your best efforts. Now is the ideal time to bring these parts to light - love and heal them. Let yourself become lighter and freer through this inner work. You will be happy to see the patterns that have been holding you back, recognizing that you can take the reins and be in control of your destiny.*

*Remember that the outer is a reflection of your inner world. You need to focus more inwardly and find empowerment. Don't forget that other people mirror aspects of yourself within. Don't fall into unconsciousness, believing that the other person is wrong in order to make yourself right. There can be no right/wrong when there is no one outside of Self. Love and oneness are the keys to heal and grow.*

*Those who you attract in your life are those whose energy reflects your own. The more suppressed or hidden aspects you have within yourself, the stronger the attracting factor and the more likely you will experience almost an exaggeration of this characteristic in those who you draw to you. The process of balance is ultimately the process of integration, never trying to make any quality or characteristic go away - for that is not possible. Instead, integrate that part, whether it be anger, negativity, depression.*

*Characteristics that are normally considered bad in society are just part of the whole. In the process of becoming whole, it is necessary to embrace those aspects by sending love to those aspects. Not accepting or being afraid of any of these qualities will simply give them power over you and keep yourself separated. Only in loving them can they transform into higher qualities.*

# Inner Child Healing

On this journey to soul embodiment another key part to heal and integrate is the inner child. The inner child is your emotional self. You have always had this part of you. Although your physical body has developed and changed over the years, you never outgrow your inner child. No matter what age, 25 or 80 years old, you will always have an inner child. This is actually a blessing!

Modern society places little value on the emotions. Emotions are the unsung heroes of the psyche. Perhaps you've been thinking, "If only those pesky emotions would leave me alone, then I could have peace of mind. I could easily become the master of my Self. It would be so much easier to focus my mind and be in control. "

Sure, emotions are at times inconvenient and unpredictable, but they also are what make you gloriously human. Take away all your emotions and you are basically a limited edition, inefficient flesh and blood robot. Not only do emotions color and contextualize your experiences, but they also can serve as powerful instruments for self-healing.

Emotions are a diagnostic tool. Emotional pain can signal that something in your life is out of balance, much the way physical pain does. If you place your finger on a hot stove, pain tells you that something is wrong and to move your finger. It'd be a much bigger problem if you just took a painkiller but left your finger on the stove. Pain can be a useful indicator that something needs to change.

If you frequently experience emotional pain, it could be signaling to you that your thoughts or your actions are not aligned with your heart's desire. You may think outside events cause your emotions. If someone slapped me, I might say, "You made me sad because you slapped me." But if she slaps my friend, my friend could say, "You made me angry because you slapped me!" The reality is that no one and nothing can force you to feel a certain way. Your emotional response reflects the thoughts or beliefs you hold inside.

If you allow yourself to feel your emotions, rather than stuffing them or projecting them back at someone, you can begin to notice what thought or belief underlies the emotion. The more you are willing to sit with an emotion, the more empowered you become to know what you need and to know what's not working for you. As you find a healthy outlet for your emotions, allowing them a path to flow, they lose their power over you, becoming valuable tools for your journey of self awareness.

Here's a message from Will on Emotions:

*It is easy to get pulled out of balance if one doesn't have a solid emotional and energetic foundation to stabilize oneself. It is necessary to learn not to be carried away by emotions, to recognize that you are not your emotions. Emotions are helpful indicators, however, they are more useful if one sits with them. Feel and listen to your emotions, rather than getting carried away by them or instantly acting on them.*

*Powerful emotions tell you where there is imbalance within you, not an imbalance in the situation or the other person. Strong emotions generally indicate that a change is needed inwardly, rather than outwardly.*

For the longest time I had a repulsion to the term "inner child." It sounded like a cheesy throwback from the 70s, along the lines of the book "I'm Ok, You're Ok." The idea that everyone has a child within crying for attention seemed indulgent and irresponsible. I thought, why can't people simply grow up and be accountable for their feelings?

Looking back, I can see that I repressed my own inner child. It's not uncommon in a society that highly values intellect and dismisses emotions. And don't forget that trolls take away girls with big emotions! I had to first learn to value the gifts of the inner child before I was willing to recognize her within. In fact, it required a series of recurring dreams to awaken my interest in this childlike part of me.

Over and over I dreamt of finding a puppy trapped in a cage. Initially I just found the dog and wondered, How did it get there? I felt horrified, recognizing that I must've forgotten it. How long was it trapped? The dream evolved over time. I wanted to take the dog out, but the cage was locked. In another dream, the cage was now unlocked but I sensed the terrifying presence of an owner who may come back any minute and get me. What should I do? In the final version of the dream, the cage was open, no scary owner lurking, but I had the concern of how would this dog fit into my life? Was I equipped to care for it?

It seems obvious to me now that the dog represented my inner child. I've always adored dogs. For me they symbolize unconditional love. It took a few years before I understood that my dreams were reflecting back my process of integrating the inner child.

Your inner child has incredible gifts to offer you. They can bring you the wonder, enthusiasm and vitality of youth. When you take care of them, you can become childlike, rather than childish. Yes, they're sensitive, vulnerable and feel things deeply, but without them life is flat and dull. They bring depth and color to your life experience.

Oftentimes the responsibilities of being an adult begin to weigh you down over the years. You are trapped in your routine, like a robot, repeating the same day over and over. You stop exploring and playing. You're stuck in habitual thinking, afraid to step out of your comfort zone, yet longing for change.

By shifting your perspective to think of your emotions as coming from a child, you naturally know how to respond to your feelings. You wouldn't demonize or shame a child for being afraid. Nor would you abandon a scared child. Nor would you let the child run the household.

Those overtaken by their emotions are letting their inner child run (more like ruin!) their lives. Those who shut down their emotions by coldly moving into their logical mind or by keeping themselves constantly busy and distracted are abandoning their inner child.

Every child needs love and attention. Your inner child is no exception. This lets them feel safe and valued. It calms them down. You must learn to hold space for your inner child.

What does it mean to "hold space?" Holding space is acknowledging their feelings with acceptance and not judgment. It means lovingly being present with them, not trying to change how they feel or fix the situation that triggered their emotion. In this Presence, the child can begin processing their emotion. As they say, "You've got to feel it to heal it!"

The inner child can be full of raw emotion: sadness, anger, fear, frustration. Years of neglect or abandonment can cause them not to trust you. Sometimes this relationship must grow slowly. When you demonstrate your commitment by consistently checking in with them, they open up and reveal their secrets.

## HOW TO CONNECT WITH YOUR INNER CHILD

- At first, approach this child gently. In meditation or hypnosis, imagine going to a safe and peaceful place. Invite the inner child to show up in whatever shape or form feels comfortable. Most often they will appear as a child, however, they may wish to express themselves as an animal or even an object. The form in which they appear gives clues to how they're feeling. A box could mean they feel trapped. If they're a clown, perhaps they hide their sadness with humor. If they're a child, note their age because that may indicate when the wounding and separation occurred.

- Notice all of the details of their appearance. Are they slouching? Are their arms folded across their chest or are they facing away from you? Body posture reveals a lot about how someone feels. What about their facial expression? Are they frowning, pouting, smiling shyly?

- Regardless of how they appear, the key to understanding them is to ask the right questions. Always thank them for showing up. Ask them, what do you need right now?

- Be attentive. If they act tough or indifferent, don't let their demeanor fool you. Every child wants acknowledgement and love. Each time that you visit them, the inner child may appear differently. As you address some needs, different aspects may pop up to heal. Like any child, they have changing moods. Be patient.

Like any other relationship, the bond with your inner child develops over time and experience. They may not trust you at first. They may act out to test if you will still love them. Be committed to your inner child. Keep showing up, no matter what. Your continued presence shows them that you value them. Once the inner child feels seen, valued and supported, they will blossom into their highest potential. To further your inner child work, I recommend the book, "Recovery of Your Inner Child" by Lucia Capacchione.

# Forgiveness Practice

The concept of forgiveness began in childhood. You might remember being asked to apologize to a sibling or classmate for something you did, and vice versa. From these experiences during childhood, it becomes ingrained that forgiveness is how you right a wrong.

Since we're all well-acquainted with forgiveness, why do so many people resist it? Shouldn't it be second nature to us by now? Those childhood experiences can lead to a hidden belief that forgiveness is the same as pardoning or even condoning wrongdoing. There's a deep fear that in forgiving, you'll forget and get hurt again. Subconsciously you hold onto resentment as a reminder to yourself and others that you won't allow such a thing to happen again.

As you grow older, these resentments build. A resentment is blocked energy, glued rigidly in place by pain, anger or sadness. The more you allow these dark, stuck energies to inhabit your system, the less comfortable you feel in your own skin. Resentment weighs you down and clouds your vision. It's like a film covering your eyes, getting in the way of your ability to experience the world from a fresh perspective. You lose sight of the miracle of existence.

It's helpful to understand forgiveness in a new way. Although forgiveness can be an outer act in which you express it to another person, in this context I'm referring to forgiveness as inner work. It's not something you do for another person's benefit. It's not about the other person at all.

Forgiveness is the greatest gift you can give yourself. Regardless of whether you direct the forgiveness at someone else or yourself, you are the one who benefits. In this new perspective, see forgiveness as the act of letting go. "Let go, let God." You no longer need to carry your pain as a way to hold someone else accountable for their actions. That's not your responsibility. The Universe takes care of that for you. Everyone is accountable for their actions through the law of karma. It remains in their energetic system until they balance it either inwardly or outwardly.

Let go of that old heavy energy of resentment and make space for more love. Don't worry, you can retain the awareness you gained through those difficult experiences so that history won't repeat itself. Heavy emotions can be teachers. That horrible feeling tells you that choice wasn't aligned with your highest good. You can remember what you learned from that experience without needing to hold onto the heavy emotion.

Almost on par with love, forgiveness is an incredibly powerful healer.

A few years ago I received an intuitive reading from a friend. At the time, something was weighing on my heart and I was having trouble letting it go, even though I wanted to. She gave me a forgiveness prayer and suggested that I practice it for 45 days. I thanked her, agreeing to follow through with the practice for 45 days. Well, just two days into doing the forgiveness prayer, I'd completely let my issue go. I felt great! Since I'd promised to do it for 45 days, I kept going, even though in my mind there was nothing specific I was needing to forgive.

The crazy thing was that every time I started to offer the prayer, long forgotten memories emerged- the girl who made fun of my hair in elementary school, the friend who borrowed money in college and never repaid me. I hadn't thought about these people in many years. I assumed that I'd let these things go at the time when they originally occurred. Apparently, I'd just pushed them deep down below my conscious awareness, where the hurt remained buried. I could feel the forgiveness prayer cleansing my heart.

Doing the daily forgiveness prayer for a month or longer is a potent method for opening your heart to more love. You might even feel a shift in your awareness, recognizing that everyone is just doing the best that they can at the level of awareness they're at.

## BUDDHIST PRAYER OF FORGIVENESS

If I have harmed anyone in any way, either knowingly or unknowingly through my own confusion, I ask their forgiveness.

If anyone has harmed me in any way, either knowingly or unknowingly through their own confusion, I forgive them.

And if there is a situation I am not yet ready to forgive, I forgive myself for that.

For all the ways I harm myself, negate, doubt, belittle myself, judge or be unkind to myself through my own confusion, I FORGIVE MYSELF.

Here's a message from Will on Gratitude and Forgiveness:

*Start each day by feeling gratitude. Write a list of at least twenty things you truly appreciate and feel grateful for your life. Look at this list and reconnect with your gratitude at least twice a day. Gratitude and forgiveness are powerful tools for opening your heart and allowing yourself to receive love. Read books and practice daily exercises regarding forgiveness to yourself. This is how you may cultivate the love for your own being that is necessary for self healing.*

*Loving oneself is the first step towards fulfilling your soul's purpose. You cannot think your way into loving yourself. You must surrender to divine love and allow it into your heart. Again, gratitude and forgiveness to yourself are the tools here. You cannot skip this initial step on your path. Loving yourself is the universal key that will unlock all the other doors to discovering loving relationships with others, clarity along your path, and fulfillment in your work. Loving yourself dissolves and heals all wounds, including the pain of loneliness. The pain of letting go of old hurts can be short-lived if you surrender to this divine fire within.*

# CHAPTER 4

# Empower Yourself

You've been going inward to discover who you are, to become balanced, and to create love from within. What's next? You want to be empowered as the creator of your life. Now that you're getting your internal house organized, you'll need to be careful about what you let into your inner space. In order to fully embody your higher self, it's necessary to discern what's not aligned with your highest good and release, transmute or not allow it in.

Empowerment is always an inside job. You can't ask anyone to give you genuine power, nor can you ever truly take it from anyone. External power is a facade. It's fleeting and requires constant effort to sustain. Empowerment only comes through recognizing and claiming your right and responsibility to take ownership of all aspects of your life and experience.

On a spiritual path you are often challenged to take your power back. Throughout history, people have abused power for control and domination. The word empower, however, has a positive meaning of giving power. The spiritual transformation we are living through is a collective shift into our individual empowerment.

Like many others, I've been working through layers of these themes for years, and so my spirit guide Will has given much guidance on these themes.

Here's a few helpful messages from Will on Empowerment from Within:

*It is necessary that each human being comes into alignment with their soul's essence. When you have taken on qualities that do not match your essence and accepted them as your identity, you will feel discord. You will have trouble knowing your truth and finding your direction. It's important to stay on the path of self-discovery, continually peeling back the layers of patterns and beliefs that block you from the beauty of your own essence. The need for acceptance, respect, and the security of fitting in get in the way of this unmasking of the true Self.*

*Keep your focus turned inward while you engage in the outer world. Your point of reference is the Self, not the ego. The Self is vast, yet unchanging. The mind and emotions are limited and fleeting. They trick you and torment you until you have mastered them as tools of the Self. The mind and emotions are not you, nor are they your enemies. Guide them well and they will serve you well on the path of self awareness.*

\*\*

*You are learning how to be strong and trust yourself despite others' reactions. Above all you mustn't lose faith in yourself due to others' disregard or disrespect. Know your worth and don't let anyone talk you* down. *When you have a strong unshakable knowing of your value and worth, you will stand up for yourself despite the backlash you may receive from others, rather than cowering down, feeling hurt and defeated as you've done in the past. No one can take away your sense of self worth. Recognize that in every circumstance you have given it away. Decide to take back every ounce of self worth you have ever given over to another in any circumstance. Then you will truly feel empowered.*

*Your empowerment does not depend on the situation; it depends on your choice. No matter how heartbreaking this circumstance, no one can ever take your empowerment or your worth from you. To be fully happy and complete, each individual must come to recognize that no one can give them their self worth nor take it away. You are stronger than you have given yourself credit for. Accept your inner strength and wear it proudly like a badge of honor. It's time to stop playing small and to shine your light fully.*

**

*Let your own personal reality be that of unconditional love and support for yourself and for those whom you come in contact with. Your own shifts assist the planetary shifts. Focus on where you can do the most good within your own sphere of influence. No good act, however small, is forgotten. All love feeds into the greater divine source of love which returns back to you greatly amplified.*

*Focus primarily on your intention. What energy do you want to radiate? Let the energy guide you to the behaviors and thoughts that are aligned with it. Naturally this will lead you to the outcomes and possibilities that are aligned with the energy you radiate. It is that simple, yet it takes constant awareness to master. Let yourself be free to make mistakes, continually bringing your awareness back to which energy you want to radiate. Eventually life becomes simpler, more joyful.*

*Focus within, on your own inner reality. Allow others to learn through their dramas, without needing to fix them, without needing them to conform to your way of being. You all have a unique path to follow. Each soul is beautiful in their own authentic expression. No one needs further instruction once they have connected to their Divine Inner Light and live from this space.*

**

*Recognize that some people may not appreciate what you have to offer. Make peace with this idea. And then focus on those who do appreciate who you truly are. There is no rule that says you have to pay attention to everyone else's opinion. Each person has their own unique truth based upon their beliefs and past experiences. Those with similar truths to you will naturally appreciate you more and understand you.*

*Do not waste your time trying to change other people's truth. Use your awareness and energy simply to recognize those whose truth complements your own and become friends and acquaintances with these people. You cannot always control who you spend your time with, however, you can control who you focus your energy on.*

In this section you'll learn practices that empower you as a creator of your reality by consciously choosing which energies, thoughts, and behaviors to engage in.

# Master Your Mind

Healing, clarity, and divine connection are not completely satisfying if you feel you lack the inner authority to create change in your life. You are raised to believe in an external power structure. What's right and wrong has been dictated by outer authorities - your parents, your teachers, the church, the government.

Your thoughts plus your emotions, fueled by your vibration, manifest your reality. It's important that you recognize the immense power of your mind and learn how to best utilize this tool. In previous chapters, I already covered how you can begin to develop emotional and energy mastery. Now it's time to explore the mind. Establishing a healthy mindset will transform your experience of the world.

## Clear Out Old Programming

True healing begins when you take ownership of your beliefs, thoughts, and feelings. Many of your beliefs were ingrained in you from your family since birth. As a child, you were a sponge. You soaked in these ideas from your trusted caretakers and authority figures, mostly without evaluating them. Because you assumed these beliefs to be true, life reflected it back through your experience in a self-fulfilling prophecy. In this way, your beliefs solidified into certainties.

This isn't about blaming your parents or caretakers. They were socialized in the same way. These patterns have been passed on perhaps for many generations. Over time you collect a variety of sometimes mismatched or conflicting ideas about life. In addition to the beliefs you're given, you also develop inner programming in response to perceived successes and failures in your life. This process occurs subtly for most people, without conscious awareness.

Many people are bound in chains of beliefs, imperceptible to them because they see them as truths. Beware of becoming a slave to any ideology. As an adult, it's best to carefully and regularly evaluate your core convictions and let go of the ones that no longer serve you. This requires paying more attention to the constant inner dialogue running in your head. Practicing mindfulness, a mental state that involves being fully focused on "the now," will greatly enhance your ability to notice these unhealthy thought patterns in order to change them.

Here's a message from Will on Releasing Patterns Through Mindfulness:

*How can you let go of old patterns? Become conscious, then you will have the freedom to make a choice that fulfills you. Any moment lived without awareness, without being in the present moment, allows the subconscious to be in control. In each moment that you are present, you can make a conscious choice to follow your heart and what feels good.*

*Do those old patterns feel good? We bet they don't. They only have power when you relinquish control by not being in the moment. In this moment there's no past and no future. When you are present, you are free to follow what feels best right now and allow the mind to navigate the path.*

*How can you be in the present? Your body always lives in the present. Be aware of your breathing or use your senses to allow you to fully experience this moment. You may discover there is more joy in just BEING than you ever experienced before. The process of being and allowing is the ticket to your freedom. So simple and yet so powerful.*

Hypnosis is another effective method for uncovering subconscious limiting beliefs and replacing them with empowering thought patterns. Hypnosis can be practiced with a trusted professional, or you can easily learn self hypnosis online or with a book. You could also simply write a list of wherever you feel stuck in your life and what beliefs are connected to it. Rewrite the disempowering statement into a new positive statement that you use daily as an affirmation. For example, change "I never have enough money" to "I receive from the infinite abundance of the Universe." Will has another useful method below.

Here's a message from Will on Transforming Belief Filters:

*There is a need for you to look at past behaviors and belief systems. Use this opportunity to acknowledge which thought patterns and beliefs do not serve you. Which ideas bring joy and fulfillment? Which ideas bring sadness and despair? Recognize that it is the ideas and beliefs that cause your emotional state, not the events that have occurred in your life.*

*When you can pinpoint which thought patterns are creating your pain and discomfort, you are then empowered with the ability to choose different thoughts. You could say that this is the "reason" these events occurred in your life, as an opportunity to mirror your own beliefs systems back to you. You actually draw your experiences to you based on resonance in energy fields. Even so, the way you perceive an event can change instantly by bringing your awareness to what beliefs you use as a filter for your experience.*

*Become aware of how drastically your emotional state varies depending upon your belief filter. For instance, if you believe a person was drawn into your life to open your heart to feeling love, that brings about one emotion. Now imagine that meeting this person was a random, meaningless occurrence. How does that make you feel? What if you believe that you do not deserve love and happiness? How does that make you feel? What if you believe that love relationships distract you from your true purpose in life? How do you feel now?*

*Notice that we do not focus on what is the "true reason" behind this experience. Instead, we focus on what is your perception of this experience. Your perception is always your truth. All perceptions are part of the one truth. Each individual is here on earth to experience a particular focus that is their truth. The key is to look at your perception and evaluate whether it is serving your experience. If you are not satisfied with your experience, it is a signal for you to change your perception.*

*When you change your perception in a way that brings about the satisfying experience, you will radiate positive magnifying energy. This energy will draw more things of the same vibration to you. Regardless of the resonance of any person, thing, or event, your perception will create your final experience. This is why two people can experience the* same event very differently. You have the ultimate empowerment and responsibility to choose your beliefs and therefore your perception.

How about a homework assignment? For the next 24 hours, keep a pen and notepad with you wherever you go. Once every hour, note your emotional state and the thoughts you were thinking at the time. If you are dissatisfied with your emotional state at the time, examine the thoughts you were thinking. Come up with at least five different ways of looking at the same idea and write them down.

For instance, if you are feeling depressed and you are thinking, "I have no energy to do anything." What are some other ways of perceiving this idea? Perhaps, "I am reserving my energy for future use." "I am using my energy for introspection and self healing." "I will seek outside assistance to restore my energy." "I choose healthy habits such as eating well and getting enough sleep to restore my energy." Notice that there are many positive options to choose from. Of course, there are many negative options that we did not mention. Find the one idea that will serve you best and begin to focus on it or put it into action, if possible.

Repeat this exercise throughout the day. Notice how often thoughts come up that are related to past events. This exercise is excellent for healing the past. You have the power of awareness to heal the past. All time exists simultaneously. It is the focus of your awareness that creates the past or the future. This focus of awareness empowers you to create a new past or a new future through your perception, which is shaped by the beliefs you choose.

It is time for you to consciously use your mind and awareness for its intended purpose - to bring light and healing to yourself first, and then to others. Through overcoming these obstacles first within yourself, you will then have the tools to be of service to others.

# Quit Trying to Be Perfect

Perfectionism is one of the most common and pervasive roadblocks to fulfillment that I encounter in my clients. To all you perfectionists out there, I have bad news: It's impossible to be perfect throughout this human experience. You're going to mess up sometimes.

There will be little mistakes and also big ones. Guaranteed. Add one more to the list of life's certainties: death, taxes AND mistakes! Since it's inevitable, why not accept it? Take it one step further and even embrace it!

What if you could shift your perspective to see mistakes as being not only natural, but also an essential part of the growth process? What if the whole purpose of being human was to learn through trial and error?

If you always did everything perfectly from start to finish, the chart of your life would be a flat line. No growth. You would not be much different from a machine. Everything would happen as you already knew it would. There would be no spontaneity, no surprises.

Where's the fun in that?

The thrill of being alive comes from the unexpected. Taking a step and not knowing where it will take you. Sometimes it will lead you somewhere amazing. Other times you will fall flat on your face. Expect that. It's part of the growth process.

Once you accept that there will be missteps, it's much easier to pick yourself up after a fall and have a laugh about it. Then the next time you will step around or try walking in a different direction. That's growth!

Isn't growth part of your life purpose? Everyone is so different and yet the underlying essence of whatever you're trying to achieve is growth. Whether you want to grow your bank account or grow your heart to love more, you have to experiment through trial and error to break the barrier of where you're at now and level up.

That seeming failure gives you fresh insight that was inaccessible before that experience. It's not enough to intellectualize something and live in your head. You learn through the visceral experience. Who are you going to trust more: the doctor who got the best exam scores but hasn't had contact with patients, or the one who also did a couple years of residency?

It's not a mistake if you learn from it.

Turn lemons into lemonade by releasing fear of failure, embracing mistakes graciously, and growing from the experience. Your life will transform!

Here's a message from Will on Facing Fear:

*There is no reason to be afraid ever. No one can truly take anything of value away from you that you do not offer freely, regardless of whether it is your self-worth, your dreams and ambitions, or your joy and peace. These things are available to you in abundance if you keep yourself open to them. They come most easily when you are connected to the divine qualities of love and acceptance, rather than the smaller personal characteristics of self importance, worry, or fear. These last qualities hold a lower, limiting vibration that does not vibrate in the same frequency as the higher qualities and therefore, cannot hold those energies.*

*You have done an excellent job of recognizing the falsehood in your limiting beliefs. Now all that is needed is to experience the truth, so that you can become one with it. This requires great courage. Letting go of the old familiar ways and stepping into the unknown can be frightening. There is no easy way, you must just do it. Only the repeated experience of trying and surviving your attempts will assure you that it is indeed safe, albeit a bit scary.*

*The issue is not to try to dissipate the fear, nor to run from it. Allow it, face it, make friends with it. Only when you disassociate from your fear or shrink from it, does it gain power over you. Get comfortable with your fear and then nothing can ever hold you back again.*

# Intention Vs. Expectation

Have you ever noticed how your expectation of something affects your experience of it?

As an avid world traveler, I'd been told for years by random unrelated people in various countries, "You need to go to Buenos Aires. That city matches you. You're going to love it." It happened so often I thought that surely the Universe was conspiring for me to visit this place. Finally, the big day came and I stepped foot into this hip, fun city, the capital of Argentina. I enjoyed my time there, met cool people, ate good food, explored interesting sights. Yet somehow I left there a little disenchanted.

Everything had been fantastic. There was no logical reason for how I felt except that some indistinct magic was absent. This magic had nothing to do with the city itself. It was due to this unrealistic expectation that when I got to Buenos Aires, I would somehow retrieve a missing piece of me.

Imagine if I arrived there without expectations, but simply open to any new experiences. I'm sure I'd be delighted with what the city offered. In Zen Buddhism this open-mindedness is called "beginner's mind." When you are learning something new, you are a clear and empty vessel, ready to take in whatever's given. Approaching life without preconceived notions frees you from the usual filters that muddy your perception.

The spiritual journey is full of surprises. You were raised in the illusion of separation, which led to limiting ideas of what you think is possible. As you continue to raise your vibration, your spiritual gifts awaken. Opportunities and abilities that were previously inconceivable to you begin to show up in your life. Therefore it's necessary to let go of holding expectations, which are rigid attachments to a specific sought after outcome. An expectation creates disappointment when you receive something different from what you anticipated. In this way you may miss the gift you the Universe is offering. You are always receiving exactly what you need, which may show up as a hidden opportunity to heal or learn something.

The Universe can provide an infinite range of possibilities beyond what you can imagine! Instead of having an expectation of what you want, learn to create an intention, which is a desire without attachment to the outcome. This little change in your mindset can completely transform your experience of life.

Here's a message from Will on Expectations:

*Stay positive yet try to remain free of specific expectations. This can seem like a contradiction at times. Recognize that many times you are dissatisfied due to your own expectations, while you feel pleasantly surprised when you remain free of expectations. It is a challenge to walk forward without seeing your next step, while fully trusting that it will be safe and enjoyable.*

*You have experienced moments of this trust and freedom, yet when you're not remembering this, you easily fall into old patterns of trying to steer life into a predictable pattern. When has predictable ever amazed you? You need not know exactly what lies ahead. Just be open with positive expectations, nothing too specific. You will find this way to be most fulfilling and joyful.*

## Trust and Surrender

The whole spiritual journey could be summed up by these three words: trust and surrender. Awakening happens the most rapidly and with the greatest ease once you're willing to trust Spirit and release your tight grip. It's counterintuitive but nevertheless true: the more you can hand the reins over to your higher self, the greater your freedom and empowerment. This doesn't mean you stop initiating things in your life and just passively wait for whatever comes about. It does mean that you stop resisting what shows up.

Whatever is coming up in your life has resonance with you, otherwise it wouldn't be in your energetic field. Your life is a mirror of your energy. Even if you don't like what's turning up, accept it first and try to understand what it's showing you. Afterall, what you resist, persists! Instead, go within to receive insight and learn to take inspired action, rather than just rashly imposing your will in every situation.

Our ego is accustomed to trying to control everything. It hates losing its sense of authority, because then it feels vulnerable. The reality is that it's only giving up the illusion of being in complete control, because your ego was never solely in charge of the bigger stuff anyway. It's kind of like the car you used in driver's education. As a teenager, you were in the driver's seat, controlling the car on your own. But your instructor sat next to you in the passenger seat, where there was an extra set of brakes to step on if necessary. Your soul gives you free will to live your life as you please, learning through trial and error. Yet occasionally your soul will step on the brakes if you get too far off track.

In the past I strongly resisted the idea: "Thy will, not mine." Or "Let go, let God." I've always wanted to be in control of my own fate. "Live life on my own terms" has been one of my mottos. It still is. That motto has served me well and allowed me to develop in many aspects. Yet I now realize it can only take you to a certain level of growth and then you hit a ceiling.

During my Dark Night of the Soul, which was the most painful and challenging point of my life, I did everything imaginable to try to change my situation. I kept pounding my head against that ceiling, but it wouldn't break. I only hurt myself. The secret to dissolving this barrier was complete trust in Spirit, knowing that I was loved and would always be okay, despite how everything in my life had fallen apart. Total surrender was terrifying, but each time I did it, the results were pure magic.

The ability to observe beyond the five physical senses through meditation and spiritual practices and perceive the direct relation between the inner and outer worlds will certainly assist you in cultivating this trust. There is a degree of courage required to explore your own unconventional spiritual path, beyond the confines of consensus reality. It appears much easier to live within the safety and structure of a known definable reality. However, your empowerment, freedom and authenticity is a hefty price to pay for that comfort.

Why not start small in trusting Spirit by letting your intuition guide you for little things, like which route to drive to work or whether to take an umbrella? As you take note of how often your intuition is helpful, you may then expand to bigger things, like where to go on vacation or where to live. Trust in your higher self can develop just like trust develops with any other relationship: over time and with experience.

# Listen to Your Heart

We humans are funny creatures. We often run from the things we most desire and chase the things that don't fulfill us. If we are honest with ourselves, we can admit that we all want to be seen, understood and loved for who we are inside. Being appreciated for outer things like achievements or looks gives you fleeting fulfillment, as well as pressure to continue to produce more to receive further recognition. It's a tiring and endless cycle.

When you feel comfortable to open up to someone and they easily understand and delight in the essence of who you are, you feel joy. What a relief it is to be appreciated by simply being yourself and not having to do anything. This type of genuine connection may seem like pure luck. In fact, the key to experiencing it more is to open your heart.

As a child, your heart is fully open and often unprotected. After a few (or many) hurtful and often confusing experiences, the instinctual response is to shut the heart tightly, construct thick protective barriers and move into the security of the intellect. The intellect feels safe because there are clear rules and parameters. 1+2=3. Using the intellect, the formula for fulfillment appears simple: Just figure out which actions are needed to create which results. So you follow the formula and achieve your goals, yet somehow it leaves you feeling empty.

You are a unique being. Logic doesn't unlock the door to what makes you special; only your heart knows what lights you up inside. How could society's cookie cut norms perfectly fit the one-of-a-kind puzzle piece that you are? When you engage in life from your heart, you experience the cold world coming alive again. You reawaken your childhood wonderment. You realize that life is not uncaring; you have simply shut down the pathway to the love, joy and passion available through the heart.

In actuality, the mind and the heart need each other. Rather than being adversaries, they can work together to provide a counterbalance. The mind gives definition to the self, providing focus and direction for the heart's flowy expansiveness. The heart humanizes the cold logical mind, creating opportunity for connection by softening its rigid isolationism. Together they form a powerhouse for your fulfillment. Let the heart be your compass and the intellect be the navigator. The heart points the way to your happiness.

Here's a message from Will on How to Trust the Heart:

*The life experience is ripe with choices. Each moment provides the opportunity to choose what to think, what to feel, and what action to take. In each moment, allow the heart to first register the feeling-tone, then the ego-mind can find the course that brings the most joy and fulfillment.*

*How can you allow yourself to trust your own higher consciousness, as well as the greater divine consciousness, over your own ego-mind? The ego has served you the best that it could for all these years. We don't wish to downplay its abilities or significance in the role of organizing tasks and getting things done. It has many specific attributes that can be applied to any area of your life to create successful completion of goals and objectives.*

*What the ego-mind cannot provide you with, however, is happiness. Let's look at a spoon, which is an excellent apparatus for picking up food, but not for cutting the food. A knife is perfectly suited for cutting the food. In rare instances, you might possibly cut up some food with the spoon using much effort and achieving little precision. The ego-mind is a tool much like a spoon, with its specific function. This tool works spectacularly for filtering, analyzing, clarifying, and categorizing information, as well as charting possible pathways.*

*So what is the tool for experiencing joy and fulfillment? You can probably guess, it is the heart. The heart allows you to feel what is aligned with your spirit. When your heart is full of love and joy, you can be sure you are aligned with your higher purpose and soul's direction. Both tools are necessary and useful. You should not rely on just one or the other. They are meant to work together to support your soul in experiencing that which it came to earth to experience. The challenge is to use each tool for its intended function.*

*Modern society has placed the ego-mind on a pedestal and given it almighty powers. It fulfills all roles in the decision-making process. Instead, allow the heart to first determine what brings joy and light to your being. Once that has been determined, it is the ego-mind's role to do its job of analyzing and sorting data to chart the course.*

*This process applies just as much to your spiritual growth as to your choice of profession or everyday concerns. Apply this process to small decisions first. "Do I want to eat an apple or a pear? What feels better? What brings me more joy?" This is the heart first. Then if the heart de-*

cides the apple brings more joy, let the mind determine the logistics - how to prepare the apple, how much to eat.

As you practice this process with small decisions, you will begin to trust its effectiveness. At that point you may wish to apply it to increasingly bigger decisions. Through this experience you can build your confidence in your own ability to make choices that are both wise and joyful. This is essential for finding inner peace and fulfillment.

There is an inherent distrust that has developed between the heart and the mind. Most people have followed their heart at least a few times and been deeply hurt. This created a fear and lack of trust in the heart. And so they decided to rely on the cold logic of the mind, yet found emptiness and dissatisfaction. These tools need to work in tandem to create a beautiful system of checks and balances. Once you begin to apply this practice to your life, you will discover that you have a fine-tuned inner navigational system, worthy of guiding you through the hills and valleys of everyday life. You could never be lost, unless that is a choice you allow yourself to make.

# Energy Hygiene

You can't be a master of your Self without becoming a master of your energy. Learning simple tools for managing your energy will help you take your power back in any situation. Although I've been an energy healer for many years now, I'm embarrassed to admit that I've only been practicing daily energy hygiene for the past couple years. What exactly do I mean by energy hygiene? Regular practices, such as grounding, aura setting, aura protection and aura clearing, that keep your energy field clean, stable and unaffected by the surrounding energies.

It wasn't like I never did these things all these years. I sometimes did them when something felt off. When I felt shaky, spacey or in some way unstable, I would ground. If I felt weird after being around someone, like I'd picked up their energy, I'd do aura clearing and protection. I don't know why it took me so long to realize that these practices should be preventative care for my energy system, rather than treatment.

Afterall, you don't just brush your teeth when you have a toothache, right? You brush daily to prevent tooth issues. This is why I call it energy hygiene, similar to dental hygiene. It's something you need to do daily to maintain your energy body's health.

You've probably heard a million times, "You can't control everything around you, you can only control yourself." Learning how to take care of your aura, your energy field, is how you can be in control of what you experience despite the environment around you. Think of your aura as being like your energy body home. It feels good to have a clean and tidy home. You keep your door shut and locked to protect your space and keep intruders out.

# Grounding

Grounding is incredibly helpful during this time of global instability. What is grounding? My simple definition is: keeping your mind and awareness in your body. It's being in the present moment. All of your fears and anxieties do not exist in the here and now; they are future oriented. The physical body is your grounding tool. It's the foundation you build your energetic house upon. Unlike your mind, emotions or energy, your physical body is always here in the present moment. So if your body is healthy and you stay present in your body, you are automatically grounded. Your body is like the root system of a tree. It keeps you connected to and supported by the Earth, grounded in this moment.

A key step for grounding then, is to take care of your physical body. Common sense daily practices for taking care of your body are: getting adequate sleep, eating healthy whole foods, regular exercise, drinking enough water, spending time outdoors and managing your stress levels.

Signs that you are ungrounded include: spaciness, headaches, dizziness, nausea, anxiety, shakiness, bumping into things, being overly emotional or just an inner sense of being not quite right.

As you stay centered in your body, you feel calm and stable. Practicing even 5 or 10 minutes of grounding can be highly beneficial. It's a great way to start your day and minimizes your reactivity to outside forces like the news and social media.

Here's some suggested practices to help you ground:

1. Take care of your body. Get enough sleep, exercise, eat healthy food and hydrate. This is the first crucial step. If you are sleep deprived or going through sugar highs and lows,

you will feel unstable and be more susceptible to worry and fear.

2. Spend time in nature. Nature is incredibly calming and grounding. Your body and mind slow down and align to the rhythm of Mother Earth.

3. Mindfulness meditation. Mindfulness is perhaps easier than other types of meditation because it doesn't have a complicated technique and can be practiced anywhere. You simply scan your body and notice what you're sensing and feeling. This brings your energy back to your body and helps center you. Headspace is a good free app that can guide you through this.

4. Mind/body practices such as yoga or meditative martial arts keep your awareness in your body and naturally ground you. There are a lot of great free videos online.

# Aura Setting

A key to developing healthy energy hygiene is learning how to establish and maintain your aura, your personal energetic space. Your aura is the container of your energy body that you carry with you everywhere you go, like a turtle carries its home on its back. Most of us are not even aware of our aura, or pay little attention to how it's set. That's like not bothering to notice whether your front door is left open or if it's locked. If you're not paying attention, unwanted energies or emotions from other people or situations can come in.

It's important that you learn to set your aura at a comfortable, appropriate space surrounding you. Let it be resilient and vibrant so that you're not easily susceptible to other people's energy and emotions. You've probably noticed that when you're on social media, when you go to work or are around certain family members, other people's energy can easily affect you if you're not careful. You often pick up other people's emotions without realizing it and then experience it as if it's your own. To truly know your Self, you first need to clean up your energetic space and become more aware of what's your stuff and what's other people's stuff. You don't need to be taking on other people's stuff. It's not healthy or helpful.

You can imagine your aura like an energy bubble around you. A healthy base point for your aura is about 2 ½ to 3 feet around you. If you're someone who tends to be more closed off, you may need to stretch your aura out. If you tend to feel other people's stuff and are more open, you'll need to pull your aura in. You do this simply through visualization, imagination or intention.

Once you've established your aura boundary, set it with the intention that only supportive energies flow in. Unsupportive energies gently bounce off.

Don't worry if you can't see or feel your aura. Energy follows intention. Simply by setting it this way each day, it will begin to form in a new healthy way. You may wish to tune into it and fortify it before any situation where you find yourself easily affected by others' energy, such as going into big crowds, attending important meetings or spending time with difficult people.

# Aura Protection

Now that you've set your aura in a healthy place, it's necessary to also safeguard it. Aura protection is like locking the door to your energy body house. The easiest technique for securing your aura is to place a protective layer of energy around it, like a bubble of light. It's common to use white light or golden energy. You can also choose numerous other colors such as blue, which is Archangel Michael's color, or rose gold, which is a Christ Consciousness color.

With your auric bubble in place, the door is locked and you can choose who you allow in. You do this by setting your intention: "Only that which aligns with my highest good may enter or remain within this boundary. All else must move outside of the boundary or transmute into the Violet Flame as they so choose." The Violet Flame is a tool for transforming lower energies into higher vibrations. You'll learn more about it in the next section. You can state your protective intention however you'd like, as long as it's not harmful to others and honors everyone's free will.

Here's a message from Will on the Bubble of Light:

*Each day in your imagination, perhaps in the morning or anytime before you will come in contact with a person who affects your energy in* a strong way, imagine this bubble around you. This bubble only allows in what you want to allow and what doesn't feel good can simply bounce off the bubble gently and harmlessly. This is a wonderful tool for becoming more aware that you can completely control how you feel, what you think, and what you allow to affect you.

Even though there are expressions like "You make me so angry," the reality is "I allowed you to make me angry." "I have unconsciously chosen to become angry." No one can make you angry unless you allow it to happen. Using the bubble helps as a conscious reminder and a tangible means to choose what you allow into your energy field and to keep out what you don't want.

It's also important to realize that each person can perceive the world in their own way. They are in fact living in their own bubble. Each bubble can have its own truth. It's not necessary that we perceive things in the same way as those around us. Each person will perceive in the way that is right for them at this time. So some may have a very negative outlook and that is where they choose to be at this time. If and when they want to change that, they can and will do so. It may never happen. Therefore, you only have control over what you perceive and what you allow in your bubble. Trying to control what others perceive will be very tiring and frustrating and ultimately not useful for you or them. If the person wants to change and wants your help, they will ask for it. They cannot change you. You cannot change them.

# Aura Clearing

The last piece of energy hygiene is to clear your aura. Just like your home, it needs regular cleaning. There are endless methods for clearing your energy field. Rather than overwhelm you, I'm going to describe three of my favorites: the Violet Flame, a Shower of Light and Dissolving Cords. If you bore easily, you can research the many other ways or even make up your own technique. Remember, energy follows intention, so whatever you imagine inwardly does affect your aura.

- The Violet Flame is a high vibrational spiritual energy that can burn through impurities. It alchemizes lower energies into higher ones. To use the Violet Flame, imagine a giant violet-colored fire the size of your aura. If you are not great at imagining, you can simply intend that the Violet Flame runs through your aura. Remain in the transmuting Violet Flame for one or two minutes initially, removing the violet flame with your imagination or intention when you finish.

- Shower of Light Method - Imagine a rain shower made of golden liquid light pouring on and through your aura. Let it rain at least two to five minutes. You can even practice this method when you're physically in the shower.

- Dissolving Cords Technique - You have energetic cords with everyone you're closely connected with. These strands of energy allow thoughts, emotions and psychic information to transfer between you. Healthy cords are based in unconditional love, without judgment or expectation placed on one another. Unhealthy cords can transmit negative energy or take energy from another. Most of the time people are unaware of the negative cords they plug in to you. Nonetheless, it'll still drain you. Don't get upset because you may unconsciously be doing the same to others. You'll want to clear these types of cords by dissolving them.

If you are open to the idea of working with Archangel Michael, you can call on him to clear any unhealthy energy cords for you. Archangels are divine eternal beings that operate in the physical world to protect, inspire and serve humanity. Another method would be to imagine having a light saber like Luke Skywalker's that you run along the perimeter of your body with the intent of dissolving negative cords. Or you can just use your intent: "I now clear any energetic cords attached to me that are not aligned with unconditional love. I give back other people's energy and I take back my own energy, cleansed in white light. So be it."

Here's a message from Will on Energy Hygiene:

*Now is a potent time energetically. You are highly sensitive, so you must take care to find the proper balance to not overwhelm your delicate energetic system. Enjoy this time but also remember to set healthy boundaries for yourself and don't be afraid to express your needs clearly. Others may mean well but simply don't understand how you are affected so strongly. Try not to get upset. Simply take precautions to care for your body and for your energy. It is an important lesson in the coming months and years, as your energy will constantly be subjected to higher frequencies and will more easily be affected by these energies than some others will. As always, seek balance in all things. The path of moderation suits you best.*

# Healthy Boundaries

As you embody more of your divine self, which exists in oneness, that means there should be no boundaries between you and others, right? Uh, no. Not quite. It sounds logical, but I don't recommend it. You incarnated in a physical body to experience a sense of separateness to discover your Self. So you'll want to have well-developed boundaries that allow you to stay centered in yourself without being affected by others.

It's common to become more sensitive and empathic as you finetune your vibration through meditation and energy work. You begin to tap into the energy and emotions of those around you. While it can be wonderful to feel the interconnectedness with others, it also hurts to feel people around you suffering. Your big beautiful heart wants to help and heal everyone and everything. You're filled with enormous love that you want to share.

The desire to help others is an admirable quality, but left unchecked, it can drain and dishearten you. Although spiritually you are a limitless being overflowing with boundless love, in this physical body, you have a limited supply of energy and time. It's your responsibility to yourself to learn to manage your inner resources.

The energy hygiene practices you just learned are useful in establishing the limits for where your energy body ends and other energies exist. Yet there's another important type of boundary you absolutely need to put in place: emotional boundaries. Emotional boundaries help you stay clear on what are your feelings, beliefs, and needs and what's someone else's.

I know this lesson all too well. In fact, I'd say I'm enrolled in a lifelong course in setting healthy emotional boundaries.

Inevitably, every lightworker (I'm using this term to mean someone on a spiritual path) faces the fundamental lesson of establishing boundaries. Oftentimes as a lightworker, you've been sensitive all your life but didn't have the tools and experience yet to manage it. Due to your empathy and openness, you've been taking on other people's feelings, desires and expectations, thinking they were your own.

But aren't we all connected? Shouldn't we help each other out?

It helps to remember that each person is both a human and a soul and to distinguish the difference of who you're helping. Trying to fix another person's problems may temporarily make the person's ego feel better, but it may block their soul from learning the lesson they came in to learn. By being the one who rushes in to "save" this person from their growth opportunity, you're blocking their soul development.

Here's what Will has to say about this:

Q: How can I know what is the right action to take in a situation?

*Oftentimes right action doesn't look the way that ego believes to be correct. Right action involves doing what is best for all the souls involved, not necessarily for the egos. Understand that egos can still expe-*

*rience a great deal of suffering when right action is performed. The soul knows that the ego is the temporary false self and therefore any pain experienced by the ego is not real and not permanent. Thus the soul is willing to risk the temporary suffering of the false self in order to develop permanent growth on the soul level.*

*This is in fact the purpose of earthly experience – to achieve some level of soul growth. Eventually the ego that aligns itself with the soul will mostly grow through joy and less through suffering because it will not identify itself only as this limited false self. It will be conscious of its true awareness as a soul.*

So what exactly do I mean by setting boundaries? Saying no to things that aren't aligned to your authentic self. Letting go of any "shoulds" that other people or your old programming try to impose on you. Recognizing when a situation or person is draining your energy and not serving your highest good.

Setting boundaries can be scary. There's a deep-seated fear that if you don't give people what they want, they will abandon you. Many lifetimes ago, it was necessary to stay with the pack in order to survive. To be outcast from the group meant certain death. While that's no longer true, this negative belief can be buried in your subconscious, preventing you from making authentic choices that serve your highest good.

Boundaries are important for developing a healthy, empowered sense of self. Many people, particularly women, are raised to be accommodating and self-sacrificing to other people's requests at the expense of their own needs and wellbeing. Kind, compassionate people often get drained because they have a hard time saying no to those who demand their time, energy, and empathy. By creating strong, clear boundaries with others, you not only honor and care for your own wellbeing, you also teach others how they can do the same for themselves.

Being able to say no gives you a sense of inner strength and self love. It shows people that you deserve respect. When you are able to say no, your confidence and self-esteem increases. You know that each person is responsible for taking care of their own needs. By becoming responsible for your emotional needs, you are a good role model for others.

Like many things, the way to develop boundaries is to start small and build upon each success. Look for the little opportunities to be firm but kind in expressing yourself, such as with a stranger who is overstepping their bounds. Once you get the hang of that, you can move on to a coworker, friend or even a family member. A classic book that can help you learn how to speak your boundaries is "Nonviolent Communication" by Marshall B. Rosenberg, Phd. Don't let the title turn you off. The book has nothing to do with violence. It teaches a framework for empowered compassionate communication.

When you're finally able to establish strong and clear boundaries, you'll notice that others begin to treat you with higher regard. At this point, you can be your authentic self and be more capable of communicating your desires without fear of judgment. Where you once found yourself attracting manipulative people, you now find space to replace them with respectful, loving and caring relationships.

Here's a message from Will about Boundaries:

*Celebrate the small victories you are making in expressing your boundaries and standing firm, even if in doing so it appears that you have outwardly lost a connection with someone. The people or opportunities that honor and value your worth are what you want to invite into your life now to embrace and appreciate. Those that don't honor you are best left to the wayside. If you continue to stick to this plan, higher opportunities and more loving people who honor and value you will come into your life.*

*Don't be afraid of the void, as you clear away that which doesn't serve you and make room to invite in higher vibrational people and opportunities. As you continue to connect spiritually, the void will become a living place full of possibilities and excitement. It is only for those who are disconnected spiritually that the void becomes an empty, scary place. It is from this illusion that people fill the space with anything, rather than feel empty. Recognize that you have shifted beyond that illusion and celebrate.*

# Giving and Receiving

We've all heard, "It's better to give than to receive." It sounds like excellent advice for being a good person, yet it often leads to imbalance in those who walk a spiritual path. In fact, the majority of my clients tend to be great givers who have difficulty receiving. The higher truth is that receiving and giving are two equally important parts of the whole, like the yin and yang. You need both to be balanced.

If you're only receiving and not giving back, you become stagnant. The opposite is equally true: If you're only giving and not receiving, you are blocked. Being blocked from overgiving isn't better or worse than being blocked from overtaking. A block is a block. From the energetic perspective, flow is ideal. Flow results from an overall balance between giving and receiving.

Everything that's healthy and abundant has flow. The fluids in our body are meant to circulate. When they get blocked, our body has illness or disease. The money in our economy is meant to move from person to person. Afterall, it's called currency! If people get frightened and no one buys goods or services, we have a bad economy due to a lack of a flow of money. If only one person is communicating in a relationship, you are in an unhealthy relationship. To experience ultimate fulfillment and wellbeing, you need the balance of giving and receiving in every part of your life.

The archetype of the martyred healer has been venerated over many generations of history. The most famous example would be Jesus Christ, who some believe died on the cross to pay for the sins of humanity. While I believe that the events of Jesus's life happened mostly as we've been told, the interpretation of who he was and why he came is deeply misunderstood. But that's a story for another time! I will summarize my thoughts on Jesus' life by simply saying that he was a spiritual teacher who came to show us the path for our own spiritual awakening.

"Verily, verily, I say unto you. He that believeth on me, the works that I do shall he do also; and even greater works than these." -John 14:12

Jesus was trying to show us that through developing unconditional love, we can evolve spiritually as he did. But for those who believe he is our savior and that he washed away our sins, they place his martyrdom up on a pedestal as the highest path for spiritual evolution. In truth, you don't need a savior. No one does. Everyone is a piece of the Divine. The separation between you and your divinity is the illusion. You are God incarnated into form. Your journey is to remember who you are and to embody that divinity and express it through your thoughts and actions.

It's not necessary that you suffer to help others. In fact, at this point in our evolution, it's more of a disservice to others and yourself to give energy to this outdated concept. There are two paths for growth: the path of struggle and the path of joy. From the soul's perspective, both paths are valid. Your soul knows that on the spiritual plane, you are always safe and loved; therefore, your soul is more concerned with growth than comfort. It knows that no matter what happens here on Earth, you're always ok as a soul. Yet, the 3D Earth experience feels real to us, so wouldn't you rather choose to grow with joy rather than struggle?

So how do you take the path of growing with joy? The key ingredient is higher consciousness. The less spiritual awareness you have while incarnated, the more likely you will grow through struggle. You'll feel like a victim of circumstance, as if your happiness depends on what happens to you. If things happen the way you want them to, you feel successful and joyful. If things don't happen the way you want, you feel unhappy.

Growing with joy doesn't mean that you develop the ability to control your reality so that only positive events happen in your life. Quite the opposite. You will continue to face obstacles as your consciousness evolves. Oftentimes you may even confront much bigger challenges as your deepest wounds come up to the surface to heal. What changes is the way you experience these events.

It is time to move beyond these old limiting ideas that have held you back from a life that's free and fulfilling. You are empowered when you choose to grow with joy, release the pattern of over-giving, and focus instead on creating balance and flow.

# Discernment vs. Judgment

You live in a highly polarized time. There's so much shaming, blaming and attacking based on different value systems. Social media makes it easy to publicly declare your likes and dislikes, to separate into us vs. them. This easily devolves into good vs. bad. Whatever you identify with is labeled good and the opposite is perceived as bad. How can you shine your light as your authentic self if there's a fear of being judged and attacked for who you are?

In reality, no one is all good or all bad. Those are just arbitrary terms of judgment. Judging someone in this way keeps you stuck in an adversarial game of heroes and villains. To fully embody your higher self, you must acknowledge that you as a divine being have been everything that exists. Remember that everyone evolves through reincarnation, beginning with complete forgetfulness of your light, aka being the villain, into the remembrance of the truth of Unity Consciousness. In this expanded awareness, you recognize that each person is at a different stage of their own evolutionary journey, so you let go of these labels. It's the ego that wants to categorize you and others because it gets a false sense of importance in these comparisons. Your soul knows that we are all equal but different expressions of the Oneness.

As you release old patterns of judgment, please don't make the mistake of swinging the pendulum too far in the other direction and accepting every person or situation in your life. This section afterall, is called Healthy Boundaries. The tool of discernment is essential to safely navigate your spiritual journey. Discernment is a way of observing without placing any judgment. For example, I may discern that a friend has a pattern of being dishonest and therefore, I choose to let go of our relationship. I don't place myself in the role of the victim and label my friend as a villain. I simply see their behavior clearly and respond in a way that aligns with my highest good.

Going within through meditation and inner spiritual practices is the key to developing spiritual discernment. The higher your vibration, the better your discernment. As you build the muscle of discernment, you become empowered to trust yourself to make wise decisions in any situation. Discernment teaches you that it's not important to figure out what's the universal truth for everyone. Instead, you get good at recognizing "What's right for me in this moment?"

Here's a message from Will on Discernment:

*Learn to be a master of discernment. This can only happen when you are first clear about who you are, what is your energy, and what is your truth. You have the right to choose who you want to be and what beliefs you want to hold. When you find the beliefs and ideas that best suit you and the things you want from life, perhaps things like self-worth or fulfillment or clarity, then seek out other individuals who hold the same truth.*

*If you allow your truth to be valued or devalued by those who do not vibrate at the same level as you, recognize that you are giving away your energy and your power. For in order for you to receive their valuation of you, you must first lower your vibration to match theirs. Rather than lower your vibration to match another's, wouldn't you rather share your higher frequency? Connecting with your higher self by staying in your heart and seeing the world through the eyes of love and acceptance will allow you to raise the vibration of all those around you. When you vibrate at the level of your higher self, you have an unlimited supply of energy to share.*

*The credit you seek can only come from within your own heart, from your own higher self. The more that you give from your heart, the more you can receive into your heart. Think of your heart as a vacuum that will draw in the energy of your higher self when you give freely from it. Outer praise and adulation does not actually feed your heart, which is why it is so fleeting and empty. This type of energy vibrates at the level of the solar plexus chakra and is received there. Only energy given from another's heart can truly fill your heart. Yet when your heart is hardened for self protection, it becomes a barrier to receiving this energy.*

*When you open your heart to give it to others, that opening allows you to receive from others' hearts as well. Your discernment and your open heart are two of the greatest gifts available for discovering your self-worth. Closing your heart is not the way to protect it. Discernment is the way. Closing your heart is not the means to discovering your self worth. Opening your heart is the way. Fighting your fears is not the way to overcome them. Embracing your fears is the way.*

*You are ready to step into the energy of your higher self. Do not lock your limited small self up in a cage or try to throw it overboard. Fill yourself with the powerful love of your heart and watch the smaller self transform and develop into something wonderful.*

# CHAPTER 5

# Become Your Higher Self

When you first awoke to spirituality, you were shocked and excited to discover this magical mystical world hiding in plain sight. A deep, almost obsessive desire to study and absorb information on this new paradigm emerged. You read books, watched videos, attended classes and developed some form of spiritual practice to heal and transform into your higher self. Now what?

At this point on the spiritual path, your focus extends beyond just your Self, and out into the world around you. There are cycles on your spiritual path, similar to the in-breath and the out-breath. After inhaling so much love, light and insight in, at some point you want to share and give back. You start wondering: How can I connect with others like me? Where can I express myself? Who can I serve?

# Coming Out of the Spiritual Closet

It's quite common to feel irrational fear around expressing your beliefs to others when you're on a non-traditional spiritual path. You may have deep-seated memories from past lives of the fatal consequences of veering away from the mainstream beliefs: perhaps being outcast as a heretic or persecuted as a witch. Even in this lifetime, you likely experienced rejection at some point for not following the herd. It can be incredibly frightening to share your unique experiences and perspectives with others who might not get it.

As scary as it is, at some point it becomes necessary to own who you are. It's only in having the courage to live as your unique authentic self that you can fully embody your higher consciousness on planet Earth. Any way that you hide your true self disempowers you, blocking your soul's energy from expression.

This doesn't mean you need to declare your beliefs on your social media profile or legally change your name to Glitter Goddess. Although, if you'd like to, more power to you! It means that you don't let other people's opinions stop you from being your genuine self in the world. Other people are free to think you're wrong. Your soul is your guide as far as what's right or wrong for you. You've come to a place of unconditional love and acceptance for who you are, perfectly imperfect. In this state of being, you feel comfortable in your own skin. There's nothing to prove. You are simply your Self: the same person at work, at home and on social media.

What freedom!

Here's some encouragement from Will:

*This is an important time for humanity and for souls such as yourself, who have relied on words of others, whether physical or nonphysical, to guide your direction and actions. This is a time of self empowerment - a time to become fully free and self-reliant in a way that can bring you true joy.*

*This is not about being alone and disconnected from others - quite the opposite. In fact, when you fully know yourself and have faith in your own ability to make good decisions and to make yourself happy, then and only then, can you truly coexist in harmony with others and co-create in a way that honors each individual.*

*We say this very lovingly because we believe in your greatness and in the greatness of all living beings who begin to remember their divinity: IT IS TIME TO STOP GIVING AWAY YOUR POWER. This is a time when you can create whatever your heart desires, but you must be connected to your heart to do so. You must have conviction and belief in yourself and in your heart, and act when your heart guides you to do so.*

*The past no longer matters. Only the unawakened are due to repeat the same lessons again and again. Once you become aware in the present moment, you are free to choose a course of action. You are no longer enslaved by your old conditioned patterns of behavior, nor your karma - if you wish to use that term. It is up to you to create what you want in each moment. Knowing what you truly want and what makes you happy is the most important factor in creating the desired outcome for any situation in your life.*

*Let go of other people's opinions. Let go of old beliefs that no longer serve you. Let go of valuing other people's "knowledge" over your own feelings. Let go of worries and fears. Focus your energy on what brings you joy in this moment. It may have changed from what brought you joy only moments ago. Do not try to hold onto the joy - allow yourself to be created anew in each moment. In this way you are light and free and fluid - going with the flow, as they say. Following your own flow and chartering your own path ultimately brings you the most fulfillment in your life.*

# Find Your Tribe

As you embody higher and higher vibrations of your divine self, you naturally come into resonance with your soul family. On an energetic level, you attract each other like moths to a flame. This is a demonstration of the Law of Vibration. The Law of Vibration states that everything is energy. You don't get what you want, you get what you are.

The vibration you carry is what you attract into your life. When your heart is open, you are radiating the energy of your true self and magnetizing those who match your vibration. Heart-centered spiritual practices, such as daily gratitude, loving kindness meditation and forgiveness work will assist you in effortlessly attracting your spirit tribe. Follow your heart. Going to places and engaging in activities that make your heart sing will organically bring you into contact with your soul family.

Here's a message on Gratitude from Will:

*Gratitude is a feeling of empowerment and a step towards inner freedom. As you go about your day feeling grateful for what you have attracted into your life, you become increasingly more magnetic to positive people, places, and opportunities. Isn't it exciting when the Universe drops into your lap something unexpectedly wonderful? Planning too much leaves no room for these types of magical experiences.*

*You are recognizing that you are a powerful creator. Rejoice in your creation. Enjoy experiences with friends, the simple interactions that reinforce deep connections. In your heart you yearn for deep meaningful connections with other souls. You feel the validation of love and appreciation by people you respect and whose company you enjoy. This feeling state can continue to expand and attract similar types of experiences, giving you the opportunity to create a more stable, balanced outer and inner awareness. Now is an ideal time to seek this type of interaction, as you begin to decide how you spend your time and with whom, recognizing it as a key to your own fulfillment.*

# Being of Service

Lightworkers have a strong desire to help others. You recognize that everyone is connected. You have an abundance of love to give. You've transformed tremendously on your spiritual path and you want to help others to do the same. This is an admirable intention which you certainly will fulfill in various ways at different points on your journey.

There are many ways to be of service. You can volunteer for a charity. You can become a healer or another type of spiritual practitioner. You can share your experiences with friends, family. or even strangers who are open to it. You could start a blog or podcast or write a book. You can also have a powerful impact by doing nothing outwardly, but by continuing to heal and transform yourself inwardly. You are a part of the Oneness. Any spiritual shifts you make individually also helps the Collective.

In Hermetics, there's a principle, "The microcosm reflects the macrocosm." It basically states that there is a direct correspondence between the part and the whole. If there's an infection in your finger, it affects the whole body's health. When the finger heals, the entire body benefits. In the same way, when you as an individual heal, all of humanity benefits.

As each of us increases our vibration through inner work, higher vibrations become more accessible for everyone on Earth. Try not to overthink what actions you need to take to help others. The path of service tends to unfold over time. You unlock pieces of the puzzle as you grow spiritually. When it's time for inspired action, you'll receive nudges from Spirit or experience synchronicities that point you in the right direction. Remember that simply being your higher self on the planet is a great service to everyone.

Here's a message from Will on Service:

*It is your path to be of greater service by connecting with more people. Reach out to others, show your Self. Radiate the love and light that you are on a bigger scale. You must be fearless in shining your light brightly. Look for ways to communicate your message and your unique energy in a broader forum. As you courageously shine your beacon of light, many more will find you and receive this love vibration.*

# Uncover Your Soul's Purpose

A few years after my initial spiritual awakening, I was feeling pretty lost. I'd left Hawaii and moved to Boston to "find myself." People always tell me I did that backwards. Apparently you're supposed to go to Hawaii to pursue your spiritual path. Well, I guess that's fitting - for most of my adult life, I've done things my own unique way.

Boston was the perfect catalyst for the next stage of my spiritual exploration. Gone were the distractions of sunny beaches, tropical flowers and friendly familiar faces. Immersed in concrete, cold weather and self-contained people, I delved even deeper within myself to overcome a feeling of disconnection and isolation in my new hometown.

The fun cafe job on Boston's posh Newbury Street was losing its charm after a couple years. At first it was the perfect position for me to explore a spiritual path. I had minimal responsibility and maximum time freedom. I'd finish work at 2:30 pm, with the rest of the day to meditate, read spiritual books and practice Reiki. I was earning minimum wage, so there wasn't any extra money to do anything else anyway.

Two years later, things were comfortable but a growing sense of dissatisfaction was creeping in. I'd made friends at work. I knew my job inside and out. We had wonderful regular customers whose orders I knew by heart. I could easily get through my days at work on auto-pilot. I was living the same work day over and over, not feeling challenged. I began to feel as if I wasn't living up to my potential. I knew I didn't want to go back to the corporate world with all the stress, politics, and pretense. Yet I couldn't see the path forward. Surely all of the incredible loving, uplifting experiences and inspired messages Spirit gave me were not just for me? How could I utilize my transformation to help others? I needed guidance from other people who tread this path before me.

Enter Delphi University. One of the Delphi University teachers was featured in a book I was reading about psychics. Delphi offered classes to develop your intuitive abilities, study metaphysical principles, and learn various types of spiritual healing. It was as close as you could get to a real life Hogwarts. Upon exploring their website, I immediately enrolled in their beginner's course, "In-depth Channeling."

Tucked away in Georgia's Blue Ridge Mountains, Delphi University was surrounded by glorious natural landscape, peace, quiet, and an unmistakably high vibration throughout the grounds.

I was thrilled to attend a metaphysical school. Even more impressive than the picturesque location and energy, were the teachers. I immediately sensed their groundedness, integrity and spiritual maturity. It reassured me to know that you could simultaneously be mystical, wise and also funny and relatable. I could see that they were balanced, keeping one foot firmly in each world, spiritual and physical.

I booked a soul reading session with the founder of the school, Patricia Hayes. Patricia's guidance was incredibly enlightening. She pointed out that when it came to big decisions, I often became paralyzed, afraid to make the wrong choice. She wanted me to understand that there wasn't a right path and a wrong path: it's all the same path! Yes, some routes are more direct than others. By worrying so much about the outcome, I wasn't taking any route and was actually blocking the natural progression along my path. She told me, "Choose, and then make it the best route. Don't look back."

This type of analysis paralysis is common in our imbalanced society that overvalues the intellect and undervalues the heart. You chose to incarnate here on Earth to learn through the physical experience. If you stay stuck in your head, you're missing the point. Your consistent intention to uncover your soul's purpose naturally aligns you with your soul's purpose. The Universe will begin to direct you to that path, but getting there is not always pretty. Oftentimes it means that people or situations not aligned with your purpose may need to exit your life. You need to be adaptable and trust that the Universe is conspiring for your highest good.

I left that first class at Delphi with a renewed faith in the spiritual path. Our teachers warned us that because our energy drastically shifted during the class, we shouldn't be surprised if some things in our life instantly changed to match our new vibration. It made sense to me logically, yet even armed with this understanding, I was astonished to come home and find that I was out of a job. The day I came back from Delphi, my boss informed me that the cafe was closing. The cafe had been in business for over 20 years. There had been no mention to the employees of any financial problems. Everyone was in shock. My coworkers began scrambling, looking for new jobs.

Fresh from my stint at Delphi, I possessed an unusual sense of calm about the uncertainty I was facing. Somehow, I just knew the right opportunity was coming to me, and I proceeded to do nothing. This time, doing nothing was not the result of my indecision, but due to trust in my inner senses. Sure enough, my inner senses got validated rather quickly. Regular customers and owners of nearby businesses heard that the cafe was closing down and showed up with job offers. I received not one, but three, job offers that week. I took a job managing a cafe at a Barnes and Noble, which also served as the bookstore for Boston University.

Now I was making more money, which could pay for all the metaphysical classes I wanted to take. The only problem was that I'd lost my time freedom. I was working a typical nine hour day, busy and on my feet from start to finish. Exhausted by the end of the day. I couldn't wait to get home to meditate. I enjoyed my job but it felt like I'd never be able to escape this imbalance of giving up most of my time at work to support just a few hours a night of spiritual practice. I would pray to Spirit every night, "I want to be of greater service. Please use me as a tool for the highest good." Then I would browse job openings online, hoping to find something spiritual that would suit me.

I don't know what I was expecting to find there. There certainly were no job listings for "Spiritual Seeker. Salary plus benefits." Discouraged, I felt that Spirit must not be guiding me because I wasn't good enough to do this work. I resigned myself to semi-annual trips to Delphi to continue my spiritual training.

During my lunch hour at work, I often roamed around the bookstore, browsing through the books. One day the title, "Work as a Spiritual Practice" by Lewis Richmond, popped out at me. When I read the title, something just clicked in my brain. I had been creating an artificial separation between work and spiritual practice. Just because I didn't work as a healer or counselor, it didn't mean I wasn't doing spiritual work. After that realization, I began showing up to work with an entirely different mindset. Every interaction with a customer, my staff or my boss was part of my spiritual practice. This simple perspective shift completely transformed my experience of work.

It's such a relief to realize that your life is your spiritual practice. Your soul's main purpose is to learn and grow through your earthly experiences. It's not a narrow and rigid path that you could easily miss or fall off of. You are on the path of your purpose simply by living each moment with awareness and the intention to continually evolve your consciousness.

Years later, I left Boston and somehow ended up in Houston, Texas, managing a yoga center. One day a student came in, gushing over a great book she just read, "Journey of Souls" by Michael Newton. "Journey of Souls" provides first-hand accounts of people placed in a superconscious state of awareness in which they share memories of life in the spirit world after physical death. I told the student, "I loved that book. I need to reread it." As I read the book for the second time, bells went off in my head with the message: "You are meant to do this work."

The funny thing is that I'd read that book at the beginning of my spiritual exploration. I distinctly remember thinking, "Wow. Michael Newton has the coolest job." But it never occurred to me that I could do his job. I wasn't ready at that time. That memory had lain dormant in the background of my psyche, patiently waiting for the right moment to activate. Everything occurs in divine timing.

As you can see, it wasn't an obvious direct path to get to my dream job after leaving the corporate job. There were lessons I needed to learn, inner qualities I needed to develop and old patterns that needed to release along the way.

Initially it's so hard to trust Spirit, but let me assure you: Just deciding that you want to live your soul's purpose places you on its pathway. Your intention to choose a spiritual path shifts you into alignment with your soul. Spirit begins to support you in fulfilling your intention by bringing up everything that's blocking you from your purpose, so that you can heal and transform it. This could be bad habits, negative beliefs, and situations or relationships you've outgrown. Having to deal with these uncomfortable scenarios can feel like you're being thwarted from your purpose, when in fact, working through these challenges is the way to reach your goal.

Let it be okay if you're not yet clear what your soul's purpose is. It will unfold in proper timing in magical, unexpected ways.

Trust and know that your deepest purpose is to awaken to your true spiritual nature while incarnated in a physical body. You are here to embody your higher self while honoring the human experience. As you continue to raise your frequency, you are helping the Collective to shift the vibration on planet Earth.

Here's a message from Will on Divine Timing:

*You lack nothing. There are always more possibilities available than time or energy available to fulfill all that your soul would love to do. Accept this first and foremost. Secondly, don't feel that you must constantly be active and busy to be contributing during your physical time on this planet. Your words and your energy can have a powerful impact on others. You could continue to be of great service simply by furthering the refinement of your energetic vibration. Yet there is another part of you that desires to manifest into the grosser physical form and this too is possible. Just remember that it is a slower process of manifestation.*

*Be patient when things do not seem to be outwardly taking shape and remember that much more is forming in the non-physical state first, before it comes into form. Enjoy this slower time. Feel gratitude for all the ways you are taken care of. You have always had enough. Now is no different. Focus on what you wish to create and how you'd most love spending your time. Let things fall into place in divine timing. How you feel is the energy with which you manifest, so spend your time enjoying yourself and feeling better. That energy will draw many wonderful possibilities to you. Things which you are not yet aware of are developing right now.*

*Divine timing is a vast organism that does not follow clock time or calendar time. It follows energy. The energy is shifting and transforming. You can feel it. Trust what you feel rather than what you see with your eyes.*

# Conclusion

So what's the end game for this spiritual journey on Earth? Metaphorically speaking, it's to bring Heaven to Earth. You are here to live as your higher self while in a physical body. Through applying spiritual practices such as the ones discussed in this book, you alchemize lower aspects of yourself and embody the higher frequencies of love and light. The outer world may or may not transform at the same rate as you, yet your experience of life on Earth radically changes, improving as your vibration rises.

As long as you're here in a physical body, you continue to learn and grow spiritually. Your vibration rises enough that you're able to grow through the path of joy, rather than through the path of struggle. This doesn't mean that your life becomes only filled with rainbows, unicorns and fairy dust. In fact, you may face even bigger challenges than you did pre-awakening. (If you feel so inclined, do an internet search on the Dark Night of the Soul. I've experienced this myself, but that's yet another story for another time.) The difference is that as you become fully anchored in higher consciousness, you have the tools and support to move through any obstacles and feel stronger through it all.

You recognize that there's an ebb and flow for everything. Your life, just like nature, has a rhythm. You accept these cycles, just like you accept the seasons. You no longer resist the winters of your life. You see beauty in the clearing out of the old to make room for the new. You're able to be in your human experience, with all of its highs and lows, while simultaneously being aware that you are an eternal being, always safe and loved.

Here's a final message from Will:

*You are beginning to download and embody the frequencies of your higher self. The merging has begun and emotional highs and lows can in part be attributed to the energetic shift that's taking place. Practices like meditation, yoga, acupuncture, creative writing, energy work and listening to inspired talks and music all assist you in holding this higher frequency. Anytime you shift into unconditional love, you connect with your higher self.*

*Keep maintaining a goal and focus to become your higher self and you will naturally be guided to the thoughts, feelings and practices that are aligned with your soul. At first the experiences are fleeting and random, but over time you will learn how to cultivate your experience so that you may maintain these higher frequencies for longer periods of time. Whenever you notice your energy and attention shifting into ego, keep directing it upward using any of the practices mentioned earlier. Enjoy your metamorphosis.*

*You can keep inching forward as you have been or you can leap forward. How about it? It's time to get rid of those false personas - the ones that say you can't make big waves, that you need to paddle softly. Try something big to overcome the habit of desiring safety. You must let go of your life preserver because it is strangling you to death. Trust yourself more.*

*Take the big chances. Even when you think you are drowning, in that last gasp of air you will find all you need to do is let go and float. It doesn't take a big effort, just a big faith in the cosmic plan. You are a piece in the bigger puzzle. Don't settle for just any place. Find the exact correct spot where you fit. Risk more and when you seem to be failing - trust and risk again. It will quickly right itself. Believe that you have a path of greatness in your own way and start living it now. Jump!*

# ABOUT THE AUTHOR

Tianna Roser is certified in a number of transformational practices, including Reiki, Hypnosis, Life Between Lives Regression, Quantum Healing Hypnosis Technique (QHHT), Soul Plan Reading and Soul Transformation Therapy. Her soul's purpose is to empower people through awakening consciousness. She uses tools and processes to help people experience their true self, the source of real healing and growth.

As a traveler of the inner and outer worlds, Tianna is passionate about exploring beyond the confines of everyday existence. For more information about her services, visit AwakeningTransformation.com.

CPSIA information can be obtained
at www.ICGtesting.com
Printed in the USA
LVHW050327300122
709584LV00014B/1969